Shattering the
Limitations
of PAIN

Shattering the
Limitations
of PAIN

Identity Restoration For A Life Of More
Like Jabez

DALE L MAST

XULON PRESS

Xulon Press
2301 Lucien Way #415
Maitland, FL 32751
407.339.4217
www.xulonpress.com

Shattering the Limitations Of Pain
Identity restoration for a life of more like Jabez
by Dale L Mast

Printed in the United States of America

Paperback ISBN-13: 978-1-6628-0143-3
Ebook ISBN-13: 978-1-6628-0144-0

Contact Information for
Speaking Engagements

Dale L Mast

Destiny Christian Church

2161 Forrest Ave

Dover, Delaware 19904

302-678-4288

dalemast@aol.com

daleandluannemast.com

destinydover.org

Facebook–dale.mast.37 & daleandluanne

Instagram – mastdale

DEDICATION

I dedicate this book to the God dreamers who have been wounded, but have chosen to live an extraordinary life filled with love and faith beyond the pain of the past. It is a high level of worship in the eyes of Father God when we step past our pain to live for Him and in Him with all of our heart. A healthy identity fuels our journey into destiny.

I dedicate this book to my wife, LuAnne, who overcame her false identity of a *"bad girl"* that started from pain in her childhood and continued into other relationships. Her mother told her *"you were always a good girl."* While it was actually true it took years of revelation for her to fully receive it. Pain is deceiving. You can read her story in her book, *"God, I Feel Like Cinderella!"*

I dedicate this book to the friends that I have, many in full time ministry, that have shared their incredible journey of passion for Father God and His purposes for their lives. It is actually breath-taking to hear their stories how they pursued their God dreams beyond devaluing circumstances and personal pain.

This book was written to help you breakthrough the false limitations of pain so that your life will be a gift to many others. I cannot tell you how many times Father God lifted my heart as I was even writing this book. Someday, here on earth or in heaven, I want to hear how Father God used your life to bring life to others. You were designed by Father God for a special purpose with divine assignments. Never allow the pain of the past to steal the dreams of your future that is connected to the purpose of your destiny. Let's choose to bring our identity from the oppression of pain into the elevation of His love and honor to reach the full potential of our purpose.

FOREWORDS

"Shattering the Limitations of Pain" helps me to understand my life story. The pain the enemy brought against my life as a young boy turned me towards witchcraft. My drunk father was so abusive to my mother I prayed that he would die. My mother trusted God, but it did not seem to make any difference. Nothing changed for her. It seemed as if God had no power. A preaching event was held at a schoolyard where I happened to be playing with my friends and he talked about the love of Jesus. After speaking, the preacher came off the platform and prayed for everyone except me. I thought he believed I wasn't significant enough to pray for. The pain and my anger raged against God. It was not my desire for the darkness that led me away from God, it was the pain.

The pain made me feel empty. The devil promised me power and promised to be my father. People were terrified of me because of the power I had, but the deep scars of pain never left me. I was paid money to curse people as a demonic Warlock. It became an outlet for my pain, but it left me empty. The pain didn't stop when I became a Christian as the enemy was trying to drag me back to him. I lost all of my income that came from my demonic witchcraft spells, so my new Christian friends made fun of the way I dressed. People doubted my transformation as a believer, but God in His love chose me to be a voice of light in a world of darkness.

People used to be afraid of me, now in Christ, people are drawn to my testimony of God's love and delivering anointing. My life has been so blessed by God that I will always give Him praise and glory. God's power and love shifted my identity from a demonic Warlock to a leading world-wide evangelist and a gifted author. This book turns our hearts from our pain to His love to reveal who He has created us to be.

John Ramirez
Author: Out of the Devil's Cauldron, Unmasking the Devil, Destroying Fear, Armed and Dangerous

Dale Mast is one of the most accurate and insightful prophetic teachers in the modern church. I have been consistently amazed by the authority and depth of his perspectives.

In his latest book, *Shattering the Limitations of Pain,* Dale shares invaluable wisdom, and profound revelations, to help answer the eternal question of "Why?" If you've ever struck a pothole in a vehicle, you know the jarring pain of the experience, and the cost of realignment, or the consequence of ignoring it. When we encounter painful "potholes" in life, how we respond is vital to our future.

Featuring the life of Jabez and drawing on our own difficult experiences, Dale carefully articulates the uncomfortable, yet necessary steps to stay close to the Lord as we await His direction and realignment for our lives...ultimately fulfilling our destiny in Him. This book is an invitation from Jehovah-Rophe, the Lord your healer, to be transformed, and to receive beauty for ashes.

Bishop Robert Stearns
Executive Director, Eagles' Wings, NY
Author: *Keepers of the Flame*

"I am so pleased that Dale has continued to write further on the subject of the believer's identity! In his new book, "Shattering the Limitations of Pain", Dale continues to rotate the "facet" of this diamond of truth to illustrate to the reader how the enemy uses the pain embedded in one's life to pervert a healthy self-image that's been given to all of us by God. This perversion causes each of us to fall short in reaching our destiny. If our heart is sick (Proverbs 13.12) there's a good chance our identity is too. Dale, you hit another one out of the park!"

Jeff Dollar
Senior Pastor
Grace Center
Author: *"Letting Go of the Need to be Right"*

Prophet Dale Mast is one of the valuable faculty members of my ministry school, Global School of Supernatural Ministry and is a great prophetic teacher. I recommend to you the book,

"Shattering the Limitations of Pain" as a great message of hope, healing and restoration.

Randy Clark, D.D., D.Min., Th.D., M.Div., B.S. Religious Studies
Overseer of the Apostolic Network of Global Awakening
President of Global Awakening Theological Seminary
Author: *Power to Heal, Baptized in the Spirit, There is More!,*
The Healing Breakthrough, The Spiritual Gifts Handbook, The
Biblical Guidebook to Deliverance, The Essential Guide to the
Power of the Holy Spirit

As I read the prophetic insights that highlight biblical truths in Dale Mast new book, "Shattering the Limitations of Pain," I personally felt old limitations that had been painfully keeping me anchored in an old picture of myself lift off. I felt my self-perception shifting. This book helped me shatter personal limitations and lift self-imposed restrictions that hindered my ability to move forward in life vision. This is truly one of the most impacting books ever written on personal identity...destined to be a classic.

Dr. Rocky Tannehill, Principle
The Tannehill Group, LLC.

Mutual friends kept telling me that I needed to meet Dale Mast. When I read his first book "And David Perceived He Was King," I knew I had found a kindred spirit. He is a true father in the faith, passionate to see his spiritual children thrive. He desires to see believers' identities rescued from their past pain. This book was not written from an academic chair. It's no mere philosophy. What you're about to read is the honest product a life lived with real pain. These treasures have been unearthed in fire.

Dale's easy writing style will tempt you to read this book quickly. Take your time. You'll be revisiting the truth in these pages again and again. Woven around the story of Jabez, "Shattering the Limitations of Pain" follows the great theme of our identity and examines the distinct ways God wants to establish it. It powerfully demonstrates how pain seeks to diminish and distort our God-ordained identities.

As believers, we're empowered to overcome even the deepest prison of pain. If you're fighting against pain's grip, this book is the blueprint for your jailbreak. Scattered throughout with important declarations and earnest prayers, this book offers a guide to deeper intimacy with God. It'll rekindle your hope in the destiny God has for you. I'm excited for you as you begin your journey of discovery in this book. I pray that whatever your pain or how storied your journey, this book will be used by Jesus to bring you to healing and into His dream for you. There is a giant of a God in you who dreams great dreams for you. I know this book will ignite a greater vision of that dream.

Pastor Greg Haswell
Northlands Church
World Without Orphans
Author: *Beyond Leadership, Pulling the King's Carriage, Finding Rest*

Apostle Dale Mast is a gift to the Body of Christ. He carries a unique grace upon His life to identify foundational roots that hinder God's people from seeing themselves through God's redemptive perspective. In his latest manuscript, *Shattering the Limitations of Pain* is a tool that will empower you to walk more fully in your God-given identity. It is revelatory because it offers fresh insight into the word of God. It is practical because it presents valuable keys that can be expressed in everyday living. It is authoritative because it flows from the heart of God through a man who has lived these truths through traumatic and difficult situations. If you choose to receive these truths in this book, your life and family will be forever changed for God's purposes!

Abner Suarez
International Author and Speaker
For Such A Time As This, Inc.
Dunn, NC
Author: *Creation Reborn, Trust: God's Unseen Power to Change the World*

In his milestone work "The Problem of Pain", C.S. Lewis faces the question, "If there is a loving God, why is there so much pain and suffering in the world?" Lewis goes on to prove the existence of the loving heart of a Father God even in the midst of a broken, fallen world. In this wonderful book, my friend, Apostle, Prophet, and Pastor, Dale Mast brings an amazing study of the Biblical character, Jabez. He brings revelation to the meaning of his name and life and clarification to the powerful prayer of Jabez that has been used by Christian disciples for centuries.

Dale is on the faculty of Dr. Randy Clark's Global School of Supernatural Ministry in Mechanicsburg, Pennsylvania, and is one of the most powerful prophetic teachers and activators we have on our faculty at Global. The revelation he brings in this book is an amazing open door to the heart of God for the hurting ones.

God has given me the privilege of training tens of thousands of believers in a prayer model that the Holy Spirit uses to bring healing and restoration from trauma and specifically Post Traumatic Stress Disorder. In this ministry, I have encountered men, women, and children who have suffered terrible trauma in their lives with many had resigned that the destiny of their lives was to carry that pain until the end of their earthly existence. I have seen what physical, emotional, and spiritual pain does to the human dream, and the hopelessness of those who experience broken hearts, broken minds, broken families, and broken lives because of pain. The good news of Messiah Jesus that he quotes from the book of Isaiah when he begins his ministry is this:

"The Spirit of the Lord is upon Me, because He has anointed me to preach good news to the poor, to heal the brokenhearted and to announce release to the captives, recovery of sight to the blind, and to set free those who are oppressed (downtrodden, bruised, crushed by tragedy)." Luke 4:18

Dale Mast has once again brought a spotlight to an Old Testament figure (like David in "And David Perceived He Was King."), and through prophetic revelation, has illuminated the deep truth that no matter what pain we have endured in this world, there need be no limitations to our destiny and the dream of our lives that God created to live out in the first place. Then, as a pastor, he provides practical application for those who still carry pain and leads us to the divine resources that our Father has provided for His children to be healed and restored of all pain.

This book is recommended for anyone who is still carrying pain, but also recommended for those who desire to be a counselor, a minister, a friend, or simply a disciple of Jesus who continues to advance the Messiah's ministry of "healing the brokenhearted." I also recommend this book for those who have allowed the painful events and situations of their lives to shape the way they think about themselves and their identity. You will finish this book believing that no matter how old you are, no matter what you have been through, God's dream and destiny that He originally created you to experience is still available for you and alive in the heart of God. I am thankful to our Father for the provision of this brilliant resource, and I pray this message will proliferate throughout a hurting and broken world.

Dr. Mike Hutchings, D.Min., Th.D., M.Div.
Director, Global School of Supernatural Ministry
Director, Global Certification Programs
Founder and President, God Heals PTSD Foundation
Author: *Supernatural Freedom from the Captivity of Trauma*

Dale Mast's new book called *"Shattering the Limitations of Pain"* is an outstanding resource and in-depth study on how pain can shift our identity away from what God's design is for our life. His use of the life of Jabez and how he attained a new destiny from God's hand of blessing on his life is captivating.

As a biblical counselor, I have been helping people for over 15years with issues of painful events that have shattered their hearts. This book is an answer to my prayer for a tool that deals with identity and how pain affects it. Dale's anointed understanding and ability to express the rich blessings associated with one's identity makes this book a must-read for anyone struggling with pain in their life or anyone who's called to help them.

I highly recommend this book for every Christian to read but especially anyone who's true identity is marred by the limitations of past and present pain.

Rock Hobbs/Pastor
Transformation Ministries School of Ministry

"Shattering the Limitations of Pain" is a book to liberate us from the effects of pain that devalues our identity, limiting our assignments. We often determine our value by the way others treat us, not the way God has treasured us. When we are not wanted or received it can leave us hopeless, or we can come before our God who created us and live in His purposes.

As a woman preacher, I was not always accepted in many circles. I am amazed how God opened doors of favor to even lead our nation in prayer, traveling to many nations as I was called to preach. When I was seventy-seven years old, God literally resurrected me off of my death bed to lead the nation in prayer again and continue building the Rock Ministerial Fellowship and preaching around the world. Never let the pain you experience limit the call of God on your life. Expect His amazing grace to pour through your life. He did it for me.

Bishop Anne Gimenez
Author: *Born To Preach, Resurrection Life Now, Mark Your Children*

God uses His love and wisdom to fashion us into the person of influence He designed us to be. Pain is a strategic attack against our identity by the enemy to destroy our confidence and devalue us. God's love for us shatters the lies that pain speaks about us. His honor restores our value and positions us for our purpose. God advances our identity to match each season of our life. Thanks again Dale, for sharing your anointed insight with us so we can rise to the next level!

Rich Marshall
Host of God@Work on GodTV.
Author: *God@Work, God@Rest*

This book is an excellent resource to overcome the pain the enemy uses to destroy our identity and block our destiny. My husband, Dale, has an amazing gift to teach with revelation that unlocks people from their past and helping them gain a renewed vision. I witnessed his prophetic gift unlocking many broken lives and bringing hope to shattered ministries. He is a father in the Body of Christ that brings healing, strength and fatherly direction. He has been a healing voice and an example to my two sons, Michael and Matthew.

As we become free from our pain, we gain authority to help others facing the same situations. His pain occurred at many levels including the death of his wife to cancer. My pain was abuse, divorce and betrayal. I will always be grateful to God for bringing the two of us together for the restoration of all things. He makes all things new. Love you always!

LuAnne L Mast, co-pastor
Author: *God, I Feel Like Cinderella!*

CONTENTS

INTRODUCTION

P ain does not build character. If it did everyone in the world
would have great integrity, because everyone has suffered
pain. The choices we make in the midst of pain will build character, limit it or even destroy it. The focus of this book is not
about building character through correct responses to painful
events, but rather how pain impacts our identity. Pain naturally
deforms our identity and devalues our worth. Our destiny is
determined by our choices that keep our identity healthy and
maturing. Our identity determines the assignments we dream
and pursue to gain success.

We can live from the treasure within or succumb to the trash
pain has dumped on our lives. The greatness of our destiny can
be buried under shattered identity created by negative thoughts
from painful events. If this is left unchecked and unresolved,
we will live under limitations that were never intended for our
lives. If we do not embrace the greatness that Father God has
given to our lives, we will never help others reach theirs.

There is an honor achieved by all of us who pursue our God-given destiny past our pain. The pain of the past will lie to us about our future. Now is the time to dream past our shattered expectations. Pain is a dream stealer, but the love of Father God is a dream builder. The faith we will need to accomplish our dreams in rooted in His love.

Now is our time to shatter any limitations that pain has placed in our thoughts and enter into a new season of dreams—like Jabez. Let's soak in His love to regain our ability to dream again. Let's lift up our voice and ask for more. Jabez shifted his identity and his destiny with his five requests and now it's our turn.

Chapter One

PAIN AND IDENTITY

P ainful events in our lives naturally induce a degeneration of our identity. We must resist it by our thoughts and words. We can shift our identity and destiny by request before the Lord. Disappointments decrease our identity if we do not maintain the value and purpose of our life in our spirit and mind, beyond the results of particular past assignment. We must address our disappointments with revelation or suffer their demanding limitations.

A disappointment can become a final judgment of our worth in our own eyes or others. Instead of having a disappointment, we are the disappointment. That is pain's lie. We allowed negative events to morph into a negative identity. Until our identity is free of negative labels, we will be stuck in the past, surrendering our influential destiny, and reducing it to an unfinished story.

We must separate devaluing experiences from our identity. If we allow them to merge, we are no better than our last event. We will lack the inner strength and stability required to expand our vision. If our identity depends on our performance, we will never reach our full potential. Our identity determines our performance. If we do not have a healthy identity, we will surely aim lower and possibly succeed. Our underrated identity cannot believe for assignments of honor.

Pain is a natural oppressor to our identity. Our identity is often created by the events in our lives. Devastating experiences can cause us to believe that we are losers that win now and then. Even frequent victories may not remove our core identity as a loser. Pain is deceiving to our value, thus it is devastating to a healthy identity. We must take our identity out of the hands of the enemy and place it back in Father God's hands—like Jabez.

We use our faith to gain victories, but we must also utilize it to cultivate a healthy identity. The enemy is a dream stealer. Past pain is his number one way of creating unbelief for our future. We must see our core identity as victorious, because Father God is. We were made in His likeness and image—victorious. He breathed His victorious breathe into mankind.

The serpent knocked the wind out of Adam and Eve through their sin and their identity digressed from open winners to hiding losers. Jesus came to break the spirit of heaviness off of mankind and break the curse off our identity to shift us back to open winners—the way He originally created us. He made us a "new creation" and called us "more than conquerors."

These terms address identity issues that He desires to resolve at the deepest level by the restoration of life through the life blood sacrifice of Jesus Christ. The great price that Jesus paid on the cross was not just to take us to heaven, but also to restore our ability to bring heaven to earth. Let us rise up and live in what He died to give us. We must never forget the power of the cross is the empty grave. Jesus is the ultimate victorious warrior—He won over death. He is winning us over to truth, breaking through strongholds of lies concerning us and our value to Him.

So we need to see ourselves as winners who may experience losses now and then, but we must never see ourselves as losers that have victories. Winners who lose expect to ultimately win. Losers who win expect to lose what they have gained. Who we are is more important to God than what we do, but they are connected in the spiritual realm.

A winner believes they will win in the midst of defeat, because that is who they are and that is what they do. Can we imagine Jesus defeated? Neither can He imagine us defeated in His plans for us. Will we experience pain and losses? Yes, but that's a temporary situation we face on our way to victory.

Faith is more effective and efficient on a winner than a loser, even though both have access before God. A blessed identity breathes faith. It is difficult to keep speaking faith from a cursed identity, but it will shift if we keep declaring truth. The results of our efforts on a long term basis will not surpass our identity evaluation. We must live in Father God to keep our identity correct and true—for He is truth and victorious. We cannot lay down our destiny for lies.

We also must continue in Father God's love through fellowship with friends in the midst of devastating disappointments. If we fall into isolation, the echo of the enemy's voice within our critical mind is difficult to overcome. The loss of significant relationships can further deteriorate our identity. Our identity will not be as easily devalued if we keep healthy relationships with others.

Perceived failures produce self-rejection if we do not maintain intimacy with Father God and others. We can often forget that painful events are a normal part of transition. Friendship is a vital source of inspiration and stabilization. Emotional pain can easily increase to anger and depression without meaningful friendships with emotional support.

It is also very important that our friends have an overcomer's identity. A complainer can never truly lift us up in our time of need. They will only provide comfort in the midst of defeat. Misery loves company—joyful lifts company. It is very difficult for a Christian who is stuck in the past to help someone else into their future.

Joyful people are content and confident. They naturally help others believe and move forward into destiny by example. The fearful soldiers of Israel gathered together each day to discuss the size of Goliath and his spear. Fear always gathers a crowd. Faith moves the crowd forward.

When David saw Goliath for the first time, I believe there was a smile in his faith—"This is my day! I was made for this." His attitude stunned his accusing brother and the doubting king—and Goliath and the Philistine army. Let the "David" in you arise. Smile at your Goliath and stun those watching.

Traumatic events can even create an identity collapse if we lose intimacy and trust with Father God, our identity creator. Our identity will languish if we keep comparing ourselves to others or their advanced position in their journey when we are wedged in a delay. The current condition of our present uncompleted assignment tries to drag us backwards into the defeats of the past so we resign as we approach our strategic opportunity set by Father God for breakthrough into a new season.

Our identity decays in an atmosphere of jealousy and lack of thankfulness, but when we celebrate others we create an atmosphere of honor that sustains us even when we have experienced a loss of authority and importance through an obvious demotion. A worshipper can never be stopped and a grumbler can never be helped.

Our identity can actually be impaired by angry negative thoughts or immobilized through guilt and shame, stealing our ability to host a far-reaching vision. Shame cannot dream effectively.

Our identity can experience glitches through lies we believe about ourselves. Truth about us produces the strength and releases the strategy to transition through disappointments on our journey of destiny. When we see our identity through revelation, hopelessness loses its ability to immobilize our dreams. *"We were made for this."*

Revelation destroys deception. The way we see Father God and ourselves must be gained by revelation. First, Peter knew who Jesus was by revelation, but it required the second revelation of the Holy Spirit for Peter to see himself as a rock that Jesus would use to build His church, especially after he denied Jesus three times. The first is always easier than the second, but the second is required to work with the first.

Until Peter saw his identity as a rock, agreeing with the words that Jesus spoke over him, he could not enter into the assignments that the Father God had planned for him before his birth. Peter's sermon on the day of Pentecost became the needed shifting point of his identity for his apostolic role in the

Church. Jesus spoke to the identity of Peter and He ng to the identity of each of us.

The depth of our identity must correspond to the height of our destiny. Seemingly insignificant self-doubts can increase to total self-hatred that can limit or totally destroy the genius embedded in our identity that determines our destiny. This genius is not about our grades in college, it is about an intuitive gift from heaven that is in sync with our purpose.

He designed each of us out of His genius, with a unique brilliance. Our identity is more important than our education, our financial strength or social status. If we see ourselves as a failure or even above average, we will sabotage our destiny with incorrect perspective of our value that defiles the significance of our purpose.

Our assessment of our identity determines the value of our life, the level of our influence, and corresponding assignments. The call of Father God over each person challenges them to perceive their identity in an elevated reassessment. He cannot use our life beyond our present activities until our assessment of our identity agrees with His. This is where we start to experience a quantum leap in our identity by receiving it from Father God—or requesting it of Father God.

I am choosing to study the life of Jabez and the principles that shifted his life in a major way. One of the most interesting factors in his quantum shift is that he initiated it with Father God. He desired to live at another level of influence. Moses was shifted at the burning bush—Jabez shifted his life with his burning desire for more.

Father God initiated a meeting with Moses. Jabez initiated a meeting with Father God. Will we? Many people want Father

God to talk to them. He is very open to have people talk with Him. He grants godly requests. Let these two verses change our story.

> *Now Jabez was more honorable than his brothers, and his mother called his name Jabez, saying, "Because I bore him in pain." And Jabez called on the God of Israel saying, "Oh, that You would bless me indeed, and enlarge my territory, that Your hand would be with me, and that You would keep me from evil, that I may not cause pain!" So God granted him what he requested (1 Chronicles 4:9-10 NKJV).*

The first and most important aspect of Jabez's prayer is that he realized the pain had negatively molded his identity. His "me" needed to be blessed by Father God. The pain that produced his broken identity was restricting his ability to possess his purpose, limiting his level of influence.

The present pain in his life was destroying his expectation that God's strength and abilities would be with him. Jabez also realized that pain in his life overflowed into the lives of those he loved. If we do not step fully into our destiny, we live in diminished returns in every relationship relinquishing our opportunity and ability to help others advance in their destiny.

Until we understand these identity principles like Jabez did, we will not have the needed revelation to make a major shift in our lives that is observable to others. His prayer is powerful because he clearly understood these interlinking issues that were limiting his purpose and assignments—diminishing his destiny.

Jabez was living in the pain of a distorted identity that would not allow him to advance into his destiny. He had a revelation that his pain was altering his identity and blocking his vision. Until we see the problem, we cannot live the change. What is around us is the least of our problems, but it will change as our identity shifts. Pain fragments our identity stunting healthy growth.

The very first thing that we are told about Jabez in scriptures is that he was more honorable than his brothers. It does not tell us that he was a prayer warrior or a man of great faith. I am sure he had faith and obviously he knew how to pray— *the prayer of Jabez*. The writer did not attribute holiness to his life, but the fact that he desired to live a godly life is clearly reflected in his prayer.

Why am I bringing all these points to our attention? These factors are always present as people experience tremendous identity shifts in their lives. Jabez shifted his life with these factors operating, but they were not the central reason for his breakthrough. Father God shifted the identity of Jabez because Jabez honored Him as the source of his identity by request. We need to have more than the prayer of Jabez; we must understand the components of his appeal that created his identity shift.

Jabez came to a point in his life where he had to make a break from his past. He realized that his life was lacking. He was not a total failure, but he knew there was a greater blessing available if he could break through the pain. Pain dismantles our voice and disheartens our will. It warps our identity.

He was not satisfied to continue living under the pain that had plundered his identity. He knew Father God could give him more as he came before the Lord that day. Jabez would not remain silent. Will we?

The writer had a keen insight into the values and inter-workings of Father God and His principles that created a new identity in Jabez. Jabez knew exactly what he wanted in his life and for his life. Jabez understood the interlocking issues that were limiting his life through a frayed identity. Others talked and dreamed about a better life, but Jabez seized it.

The Mystery Man

Jabez made a simple, yet deeply profound request of God that was recorded into the scriptures by a scribe, not by Jabez. The scribe that originally wrote the prayer obviously knew Jabez and his family personally. He chose to omit the natural details of their lives, but not the truths he observed. The request of Jabez produced an astounding identity shift. Our identity can be shifted too.

The story of Jabez is surprisingly placed in the midst of a genealogy list. His father is not listed before him nor a son listed after him. Since he was not even directly linked in the genealogy, why is Jabez mentioned at all? It seems like there was no other place in the scriptures that his story would fit or stand out more clearly.

We see this oddity occurring to a lesser degree in the first chapter of the New Testament as Matthew listed the genealogy of Jesus. He did not mention the names of any of the women except Tamar, Rahab, Ruth and Bathsheba—an unlikely disreputable list of characters, pointing to the grace of God. He overlooked the name of the well-known and honored wife of Abraham at the beginning of the list, but showcased questionable persons that came from undesirable situations in the genealogy of Jesus.

There is a huge difference in these two examples—these women are a part of the genealogy list, Jabez is not. The story of Jabez is not connected to any other historical event or people of importance which makes it more impressive and profound. His natural identity is omitted, yet a precise account of his prayer that shifted his identity is contained in these two verses, *(1 Chronicles 4:9-10 NKJV)*.

Some think that Jabez was from the tribe of Judah and a scribe as well since there was a city named Jabez in Judah where scribes lived. Some believe the city may have been named after him because of his exemplary life.

Since scribes worked together on the tedious task of recording history and meticulously copying existing scrolls day in and day out, it was probably written by someone that worked closely with him, possibly a friend or a relative of the family.

This scribe knew the prayer of Jabez and observed the results of Jabez's life as well as his brothers. The decision for the scribe to put this brief story in the scriptures was inspired by God. He must have perceived the importance of Jabez's prayer for every believer to achieve an identity shift.

The results of Jabez's prayer became a conversation among people who knew him. I doubt that anyone overheard him praying to Father God. His prayer is intimate and private in nature. If it was spoken privately, how could we know about it?

Jabez most likely communicated his prayer to someone who inquired of him. They observed that his life had shifted with surprising and notable results—*before and after.* He probably shared his story with someone who was also having similar difficulties in life or desired a shift like Jabez. "Jabez, how did you do it?"

Jabez was a man who did not want to live under pain nor cause it, so we know he was a man of integrity and compassion—caring for others as well as taking responsibility for his own life. It is very easy and deceiving for us to blame others or God for the pain in our lives as we distance ourselves from accountability, choosing to be a victim. As a victim clings to the built-in relief from all responsibility to every negative situation, they also surrender all authority Father God gave each person to escape a hopeless life. Out of hopeless situations have emerged some of the world's greatest heroes.

A victim mentality invites people to treat us the same hurtful ways that others have in the past, proving what we believe about life, more importantly what we believe about ourselves. It says, "I am not worth loving or being valued." Others simply agree with us and we continue to complain. That view of our life believes that we cannot change, until they do. Since they will not change, we can't. This is a poisonous comfort.

If victim mentality progresses into a victim identity, it becomes a permanent prison until there is a jailbreak of personal responsibility that activates better choices. Guilt or accusations are neither helpful nor needed. Father God is celebrating our value freeing us live beyond crushing failures and deep personal wounds.

We can have a healthy identity in most of our life and still have a stealth victim identity in a certain area. A successful businessman may have a great identity in business negotiations and remain in a broken identity in family relations that started in his childhood. If we try to shift the results in a wounded area of life without shifting our identity, it will distort our discernment—defiling our genius.

This is a predictable mistake that never works, but is most often enlisted. If we are not true to ourselves, we lose clarity of purpose. When we do not listen to our heart, we cannot hear the hearts of others. People then become objects in our path that we push out of our way. Destiny is lost in the obsession for success—attempting to remove the pain and regain value.

Jabez went after the source of his life of pain—his identity. It was molded by the name his own mother gave him and others called him. In the arena of life, we start with what people gave us. We struggled to create a better us, but the treasure of our genius can only be revealed by our Creator, Father God. Identities must be received to be activated, whether negative or positive—or the normal mixture of both. The mixture is not Father God's best for any of us.

When our identity is established outside of Father God's love, it becomes an idol that sacrifices others and our purpose to maintain its existence. It becomes increasingly self-centered and unpredictably dangerous in any given moment. When our identity is established in the celebration of Father God, our lives become a gift to all those that we meet. As we live in His delight, our identity enters into His creativity that develops our "me" for our destiny.

The scribe recorded that Jabez was *more honorable* than his brothers. Of all the words that could have been used to describe Jabez in comparative terms to his brothers, these are unusual words. The impact and importance of these two words are massive. Honor releases the genius within us and is a significant part of the foundation of a healthy identity. Only Father God can bring the fullness of untainted honor into our identity that launches our destiny above the grasp of the fallen spirits of this world.

As believers, we receive salvation, His Spirit, and the gifts of His Spirit to fulfill His purpose in this earth. If our identity does not shift, we limit what He can bring through us into this earth. How we see ourselves will determine what we will see manifest through our lives. His higher thoughts release higher ways. Think with Him and experience the greater.

The honorable life Jabez experienced was the result of choosing to live above the pain of the past. Carrying the pain from the past reduces the honor in our lives, limiting our influence and authority. Bitterness and honor cannot fully coexist within any person—they are mutually opposing and diminishing factors to each other. Bitterness locks up the strength of our identity and reduces us to childish emotions that twist us to speak below our level of intelligence.

Jabez entered the blessings of Father God in a way his brothers did not. Make no mistake about it, some people will never make the shift—don't let it be us. Let's be like Jabez and live from a more honorable identity. We will study the keys in his prayer, but first let's look at the mystery man—Jabez.

Jabez and his brothers were born into a situation unknown to us, but it was known by the observer of his family. By design and purpose, Father God had most of the details omitted from his story. There are stories in the Bible that go into great detail of the person's life and struggles, like Joseph and David. They serve a specific purpose.

Details of a person's life events give us greater insight into the forming of their fears and negative responses that their faith had to conquer. We can then understand better how they navigated the challenging circumstances set before them. We see the faith that was built in David's past victories that gave him giant confidence. We see David gaining dependency on the Lord's protection as he fled the murderous threats of King Saul.

As soon as we start changing what's in us, He starts changing what's around us. A life overview of a biblical character is given to us to help us relate to the person and the specific challenges that required an identity shift. It instructs and encourages within a specific context with principles applicable to all of us.

Everyone faces the same issues within unique circumstances. The ability to relate to the person or their situation in the scriptures through parallel realities is instructive and comforting to our journey of faith in this world. I believe that the details in the life of Jabez are missing by divine purpose.

Very few of us will be the king of a nation, like David, but we all have a throne of authority for our purpose and an assignment from heaven that is equally important to Father God. The fact that he was a king can make it difficult for some people to identify with his life. Yet each of us will need to exercise authority in our life, like King David, to succeed.

Not many of us will be sold by our brothers who talked of killing us, thrown into prison based on lies and then promoted to second in command over an ungodly nation like Joseph, because we could interpret dreams and had a specific plan for the next fourteen years that would save the known earth. Yet each of us will be challenged, like Joseph, to help other family members who have caused us pain.

Father God chose Jabez to be the *unknown man* for a very specific purpose. He removed all comparisons that could cause us to miss his keys to an identity shift. He gave us a particular place to relate to this man—*his pain and his prayer.*

Father God had the scribe record precise details of his prayer and the miraculous shift in his life as a personal invitation to each reader to break the limitations pain creates. Jabez had clarity and revelation in his prayer that shifted him from a life filled with pain into a life filled with honor.

We know nothing about his childhood or adult life except a few limited facts. We know he was conceived in pain or sorrow. His mother gave him a name that sounds like pain in the Hebrew language—an unbelievable identity prison. Jabez grew up with several brothers—two or more.

He was noticeably blessed by Father God when he prayed this very specific prayer. We are forced to study his prayer, not his life. His life is not the key—his prayer is. His prayer contains the revelation to shift our identity.

He is much like the Unknown Soldier who is honored in most nations. The Unknown Soldier is honored for what he did, not who he was. Honor is bestowed on his unknown life to represent all the "unknown soldiers" and known soldiers that have long been forgotten, who fought for their nation.

We do not know of the pain or sorrow that was present at his birth or the details of his blessings. We are unaware of his position in life when he called on Father God, nor the promotion he attained. The results are given without the normal numerical details, yet it is totally understood by all of us—the greater blessings.

There is no in-depth description of the limitations the sorrow and pain had created in his life, but we know they had. Jabez was limited. We know he cried out to God concerning the state of his life. His pain was deep. There are no stories of how he broke through, but we are simply informed that he did.

We do not know how God did it for him—but it was very impressive and observable to many people. Jabez received a monumental shift in his life from Father God and so can we. More is waiting for all of us.

The short account of the life of Jabez and his victory is applicable to everyone. All of us have endured hurtful situations that affect our identity in a harmful manner. The observer recording the life of Jabez wanted us to know the secret of his life—while keeping his life a secret. There can be no disqualifying comparisons here—just revelation and the invitation to experience the "Jabez identity shift."

The Pain

To be free of pain is not a denial of reality or having such a wonderful life that is void pain. It simply means that pain does not own our identity or any part of us in any manner. There are painful situations present even during the most amazing times in our lives. We don't need to look very far to find them. Jabez was not in physical pain with a need for physical healing, it was emotional pain—matters of the heart.

The time has come to stop carrying pain or allowing pain to carry us. We cannot carry pain into our future and experience the fullness of our destiny. We cannot allow pain to carry us away from our future. We must all face pain in life, but we must not allow it to form our identity or shape our destiny.

Pain changes the way we think. It alters the way we view opportunities. Pain produces involuntary negative reactions and attitudes towards life events that move us away from the success and greatness Father God planned for us. Pain lies to us and it is very believable. We will always journey past pain or the fear of pain to enter our next success. If we are established in our identity, the pain of the past or the fear of the unknown will not have the strength to impede our advancement.

Pain can teach us lessons in life, but it also causes us to settle for less. If we suffer a burn moving a hot kettle in a kitchen it should introduce us to the insulated potholder. Otherwise, we might stop dreaming what we could create in the kitchen that many could enjoy. Let's not settle for a life of cold meals because we have been burnt several times. If that pain shifts our identity, we will no longer create in our "destiny" kitchen as a head chef.

When a dream ends in the deep pain of disappointment, we tend to stop dreaming in that specific area—and the enemy knows it. Dreams are crucial to fuel our identity. Yet the greatest dream any of us will ever host almost always comes after a failure in our eyes. Judas looked like a failure to the leadership of Jesus, but it preceded a billion souls who would follow Him. Through the hurtful events that Jesus suffered before the cross, He never became bitter.

🏹 Bitterness is fellowshipping with the devil over your past. Hurts are unavoidable, but bitterness is a choice. Bitterness is a result of living in the hurt instead of above it in Him. Bitterness kills our creativity and the dreamer anointing.

Revenge is not a true victory. It focuses and believes for someone else's loss. That attitude actually releases a spirit of loss into our dreams. There is no true joy in revenge, but there is in justice. Revenge hopes to create pain for others. Justice simply believes for truth to be honored. Mercy triumphs over judgment for all of us.

Our life is hid in Christ who bought us with His love with mercy. Bitterness cannot own us, if His love already does. The presence of God within us is strategic protection from the enemy's attempt to gain control through pain. Choosing God's love is healing that activates the dreamer within us again.

When Paul and Silas were unfairly beaten up, they chose to openly praise God. It broke off their chains and the chains of everyone in the prison, but no one moved. Our "beaten up" praise is more powerful than our peaceful praise. The choices we make when others take advantage of us, will determine the power of our advancement.

Our passionate worship brings His presence. Our love for Him creates a natural hiding place in His abiding presence— divine protection. His presence journeys with us, advancing us into the fullness of our destiny. Our worship of Him within our hearts draws His presence creating an atmosphere for wisdom and direction.

"Yeah though I walk through the valley of death, thou art with me." We are never alone or unprotected, even in the darkest places and times. Worshipers are covered by His presence. His presence will walk us past death into life. Immobilizing fear is shattered in His presence. Directions in our darkest times produce the greatest breakthroughs.

A broken heart and a contrite spirit are needed components for a healthy identity. If we allow the purifying fire of God to separate our need to be accepted from the dream, we will not suffocate the dream with insecurity. If you do not understand what I am saying now, you will in your future days. Insecurity sabotages God dreams and distorts our identity.

Father God establishes more security in us as He is working through us and on us—with His eye on the greater that is still in front of each of us. We do not have to be completely whole in our identity to be utilized, but we must stay current in His process to have true authority.

We cannot settle for status quo or even the success of the last season. We must align with Father God in the next dream of our unfolding destiny that can only be accessed with a new spirit and a new way of thinking to produce the necessary quantum shifts. God dreams that shift the earth are hosted by those who are not trying to establish their value, but the value of others and the purpose of the vision. They are passionate and purposeful about releasing His light into the darkness that still remains in the earth.

If we live in pain, we are less interested in the adventure of destiny or the risk of creative vision. We must enter our destiny from an established identity with active faith and joy to launch daunting key assignments of a new vision that will shortly become our new norm.

What challenges us today will simply be the launching pad for the unthinkable tomorrows. When the Wright brothers were building the first airplane they were not contending to break the sound barrier, they were simply trying to overcome gravity. Their accomplishment lead to another opportunity they never considered; a man on the moon. They would have laughed at the idea, but actually they started the ball rolling. Never underestimate seemingly simple or crude beginnings.

When pain rules, we live a shielded life to prevent more pain. A shielded life creates a limited identity. It would be wise to have a large barrier shielding the president from the angry demonstrators, but he would not desire it in the white house with his family or in the oval office with his cabinet and staff. Shields destroy intimacy, movement and creativity.

A full body suit constructed from three inch steel plates would doubtlessly protect our lives from any shark attack, but we would lose our ability to swim in the ocean of life. The probability of a shark attack is very low, but it is also a greatly feared reality. We will certainly drown in the waters of destiny if we continually focus on protecting ourselves from all possible pain with steel plated swimming suits as our resident pain demands, instead of swimming in faith towards our dreams.

Pain is always around us, but we cannot allow it to live in us or live through us. Processing pain is different than being stuck in pain. We must face our pain and understand it to conqueror it or it will dictate our decisions and alter our destiny without our perceptive permission.

A healthy grieving process of a painful event is needed, giving voice to our emotions to release our pain. It must be communicated, understood and evaluated by a counselor, trained minister or a wise friend to help create a path to healing. We must resist campaigning with our story to recruit people to give us the right to continue to live in pain. Pain is debilitating to our hearts and wearies the mind.

Until we identify the key elements of our emotional pain, we cannot find healing. It would be like a sick patient who had a headache and brain cancer. If the doctor only recognized the headache it would not take care of the real problem, even though he may be able to mask the pain until the cancer gets worse. God utilizes pain to announce danger to our physical being. Emotional pain also announces danger to our spirit and identity. It was designed by God to make us aware of needed change.

We may have carried an issue for decades, but when we feel the pain or see the pain we create for others it is a signal that it is God's timing to deal with it. A patient must be strong enough to survive a critical surgery. Father God knows when we are ready for surgery in our wounded emotions and fractured identity. We cannot hurry the process, but we must keep current as He brings to our attention certain issues to maintain momentum in our destiny.

Pain tells us that there is still a problem that exists even though we may have experienced a major advancement and breakthrough months or years before as more feelings surface again. One issue solved does not mean that every issue is resolved from the same event.

We must first deal with the obvious pain, before we can discern the deeper hidden pain. We are not focusing on problems in our lives, but we are not avoiding them either. God's timing is a key part of the process in becoming emotionally healthy. If we try to rush our restoration, we will not correctly apply the revelation we receive in the required sequence that unlocks our destiny.

There were two significant calls in this story; when his mother called her child Jabez and when Jabez called on God. The words spoken by his mother were actually limiting his life through a repeated negative identity. Nicknames, derogatory names and sometimes our actual given names have the ability to destroy our destiny and sabotage our identity.

Labels devalue us and steal our future. They also imprint a negative identity that produces negative thoughts patterns and a hopeless future. We may not remember many things from our early life, but the painful names that people called us with the intent to humiliate us are burned deeply into our hearts, still trying to create doubt to our value.

No matter what people may call us, we can still call on God to bless our lives beyond the labels. The details on a prescription label are critically important. Labels that people put on us or we put on ourselves are just as critical. Negative labels are more difficult to shed if it aligns with a fear we already have. Damaging labels will not stick on a healthy identity that is well oiled. When we are in a drought, destructive labels are harder to peel off. We must lose undesirable labels to enter a new season.

We are not actually sure of the source of the pain and sorrow the mother of Jabez encountered. She could have actually experienced a long painful birthing process that would have caused her to give him a name that reflects pain. That is possible, but there were other hurtful issues that existed at the birth of Jabez that affected his brothers as well.

Could it be that her husband died during the midst of her pregnancy—before Jabez was born? The wife of Phinehas, the son of Eli, the High Priest of Israel, named her son Ichabod, *meaning the glory has departed*, after hearing that her husband died and the Ark of the Covenant was taken in war—and then she died. Her pain was from four sources: The *intense pain from birthing* her son, *her life* that was coming to an end during childbirth, the *death of her husband* in battle and the *loss of the Ark* of the Covenant to the enemy. Deep pain is never limited to one issue in any life.

It is probable that the pain and sorrow the mother of Jabez faced was more about the circumstances that already existed before Jabez was born, but her present pain was elevated by his birth. It is not inconceivable that the father of Jabez was already dead and his mother died during or shortly after his childbirth. I think there was a tragedy that affected Jabez and his brothers equally of epic proportions because of the comparative observation by the scribe.

We often refer to the call of God on our lives, but Jabez did something very unusual—he called on God to change his life. He realized he was living under the limitation that his mother had set on his life. The enemy of our soul can limit our identity easier through a forgotten ill-timed remark by our parents, than curses through a stranger—and he knows it.

We must honor our father and mother for our lives to go well for us, but that does not mean that we honor everything they said about us or to us. He did not reject his mother, but he did remove the label. Family labels limit your abilities and possibilities. No matter how much money is spent in postage, an incorrect label will never reach its desired destination. Unfitting labels, whether subtle or overt, are very damaging. We tend to live them, even though we despise them.

We must have a corrected label—an identity shift. It is our time to come before our Father God who created us and ask

Him to remove damaging labels from our spirit. If we try to change them through our own efforts, it is emotional manipulation which produces unhealthy emotions with survival instincts that are predictably dangerous under pressure.

We normally think of someone blessing someone else. Yet Jabez understood that it was better to ask Father God to bless him instead of asking for a particular thing. Jabez knew that a blessing from Father God would reorder his entire life, breaking the curse of pain and bring increase in every area. He trusted the blessing of the Lord.

Never let one event in our life name us or define us. Never let one event in our life determine our future or our identity. Only let the one who knew us before He created us, Father God, determine our future. He sets our future in honor, though the enemy in this fallen world plots against it.

Prayer: *Father God, I am asking you to reveal any labels the enemy or even people I love have spoken over me that You do not agree with to be revealed and removed from my identity. Lord Jesus, I am asking You to reveal to me any spoken labels I have put over my life through painful events that have blocked me from stepping into the fullness of my destiny. I break those labels by the blood of Jesus Christ that empowers me to live as a new creation. Lord, thank You for making new in me.*

Chapter Two

VALIDATION OF PAIN

Painful emotions point to the need for change. Commitment to truth is required to face the root issues. Emotional pain warps our identity and lessens our faith. In the final analysis of life, how we see ourselves—affects how we relate to others and our willingness to enter into our created purpose.

Pain must be validated by the person counseling before anyone can successfully enter the journey that produces change. It gives creditability to their person and emotions, but not their evaluation of the past event. Our assessment of past events can create a false view of others and ourselves; and therefore our future. Truth revealed over past hurtful events will release our hearts into live with freedom in our future.

Yet validation of pain should not be overlooked or pre-maturely turn into a journey to establish truth where lies are obvious. It is important to keep asking questions and validating the pain at each level to reach the root of the issue. "And how did that make you feel? Why? Where did that first start in your life? Has anyone made you feel like that before? Did your parents ever make you feel that way? Do you feel that way about yourself? How does God feel about you?

When we are connected to the pain of the event, great questions can uncover what is hidden from all eyes, but not God's. Pain can voice a truth that can be uncomfortable to admit, but it must be spoken for the healing to begin. Negative thoughts buried in pain lose their hidden control when they are verbalized. Pain in silence multiplies shame, reinforcing distrust and anger, creating hopelessness.

Understanding our emotions is beneficial to maturing. It is difficult to gain major changes if we do not listen to our emotions. They will rule us, instead of informing us. Validation of emotions creates a safe place that precedes the untwisting of the "facts" into truth that sets us free. Truthful emotions do not make our perception of an event true, but it reveals how it shaped us. Our emotions have a tremendous impact on our identity and value.

Our emotions are designed to help us respond to situations with corresponding actions with correct intensity that brings life to truth and necessary strength to journey into our destiny. Our emotions are not analytical in nature, but they will point us towards truth if we give a voice to them. It can be quite surprising what our emotions can tell us.

If we are feeling angry and there seems to be no apparent reason, it is time to ask the Holy Spirit to reveal the source of that emotion. He will reveal if we need to change or actually change something around us. Our emotions can work with the discerning of spirits or hinder our discernment.

It is often helpful to have a trusted friend or a skilled coun-selor to be a sounding board. I find that when I put my emotions into words, it actually brings clarity to me that internal thinking cannot. God's wisdom can also come through a comment from a total stranger as well as an observation from a trusted friend. We must learn to listen well with an open heart to validate others or even to be validated.

"That would be hurtful for anyone." is the needed validation statement. We must validate the pain by seeing it through their eyes. Until we see it from their view, even if we do not agree, we will not know where to start. It is difficult to walk anyone out of a place we do not understand. Then we can bridge them into truth they never recognized. We must meet them where they are to take them where they have never been.

Validating pain validates the person. It also builds trust and creates a safe place for healing journey to start. We cannot skip this step and leap into the facts and expect a wounded person to journey with us to resolve the dilemma, especially if we were the ones that wounded the person.

Defending or even explaining ourselves (or others) at the beginning of the conversation is a losing proposition since it's still about us first and them second. Acknowledging their pain first speaks of our love. Listening first to their perspective gives us insight to their pain and greater clarity of any misunder-standing or false assumptions. It also will help us locate where we should start. Listening to someone's pain and accusation about us does not imply guilt or losing the advantage; rather it demonstrates the heart of God.

Having a good understanding of their perspective gives us access to personal revelation for their situation that would have otherwise been downgraded to generic truth. Listening to others marks us as safe leaders, but the clarity of truth in our response will determine the strength of our leadership and the level of freedom that can be attained. Truth sets free, love comforts and heals—both are required for each of us to reach our destiny.

We cannot ignore our emotions or the emotions of others and win in life. If we are self-centered, we tend to overlook the emotional needs of others in key relationships. It will limit the possibilities for destiny that Father God may intend in that relationship. It is impossible to journey into destiny with those that we never connect to emotionally at a basic level.

When we find people that can identify with our pain, it gives a unique comfort. We need to do the same for others. It creates an unusual point of strength that bonds teams together as they work towards a winning season. Our identities are forged in intimate times of sharing with others.

It is beneficial to have a heart-to-heart with those who had similar experiences and learned how to live above and beyond the trauma. We must realize we are not the only ones that have experienced that specific trauma that has forced a battle for truth and healing. Others can also give us a much needed perspective that brings different truths on events that we did not see. Truth breaks lies off our hearts, pain shouts to control— even in a quiet voice.

Pain shouts and believes many things: "It's all my fault. I deserved it. I hate them, I hate my life and I hate myself. I will always be treated this way. I am not worth anything better. If I were a better person this would have never happened to me.

Other people are valued, chosen, celebrated and protected, but I will never be. Father God does not really love me."

The absolute truth is: Jesus loves me. He values me. He chooses me. He celebrates me. He protects me. He will not always stop what others chose to do towards me or what I do to myself. He did not stop what was done to Him by others. He was beaten and crucified. He always turns the evil situations towards His goodness and victories through His responses. His deep love weeps over each of us even when we reject Him and His ways. Jesus is the reflection of Father God's heart towards each of us.

Truth is more easily faced when our value is supported. All hurtful events limit us by attacking our value and our identity. Validation of emotions is a major core factor in a loving relationship. Therefore is easy for anyone to get trapped at the starting point of the process of seeking validation from others. We will continue to repeat our hurtful story seeking comfort from others until we eventually present it for healing.

We must not allow the comfort we receive from others to conceal our need for personal growth. It is absolutely amazing how God takes those things sent by the enemy to destroy us and turns them around to form our identity as we respond with a godly view towards the problem. Problems never make us better or worse, they simply force a response that forges our identity and destiny.

Our identity is a collage of correct and incorrect responses to hurtful and helpful life events. If we do not respond in a correct manner to a helpful event, it can be more damaging to our destiny than our response to a hurtful event. We are one response away from a new day and a superior identity. The motivation to climb a ladder out of a pit is an easier decision than choosing to scale a ladder to the top of a tall building. The first one is the basic instincts of survival, the second on is determined by vision and identity. A fireman on a ladder truck trains to do what we naturally fear with the added pressure of saving lives in the midst of a raging fire, endangering his own life to fulfill his purpose of helping others. Why should we choose to live safe, when we can have an adventure in faith?

The hurtful things others have done to us releases insecurity, anger and hopelessness into our lives. What we think about ourselves after those events will determine if we move on into our destiny or become stuck in that event, allowing it to disfigure our identity creating a negative expectation over our lives with a bitterroot judgment. (Nothing ever works for me. If it gets good, something or someone will ruin it. I just don't have what it takes to succeed.)

Nothing or no one can make us feel insignificant and inferior unless we choose to agree. We must break agreements with hell by choice—then enter agreements with heaven by choice. We are often about three agreements away from a value shift in identity that creates a whole new world in our lives.

We must not choose to let the hell we have been through deform our identity. We must invite the One who literally went through death and hell defeat the lies we have come to believe as truth for our anointed identity to be revealed. "All things new," starts on the inside.

Healing, deliverance and anointing are required for change. Change results from confronting our thinking and our choices. They are the only bridge out of the pain of our past into a new day of hope that connects us to our destiny.

Validation by others does not mean we were completely right, nor blameless. It simply means it would be a hurtful experience for anyone. Whenever we are hurt or offended, it points to needed changes in us at various levels—whether major or minor. The more we advance in our purpose, the greater impact minor changes create—don't ignore them. A small shift in a great athlete can propel their career to a "legend" status.

We must keep learning to respond differently to the variety of normal painful experiences that will continue to visit every heart. Recognizing and dealing with any level of unhealthy need for approval that remains in us or arises when we enter a greater sphere of honor is key to guarding our new future. The unhealthy need for approval is based in self-rejection that blinds us to our life patterns that creates abnormal levels of unnecessary drama that blocks our future. We need approval to advance, but if we seek it we undermine our value. As we live from the value we received from the Lord, the approval of others that advances our purpose will arise when needed.

When we allow God to expand our hearts and minds we gain hope that produces new strength to live above the past pain. Pain lies to us. It tells us we should and have the right to quit. Every athlete in training knows that pain signals that greater strength is being gained, but it is also a mental barrier that must be shattered. God strengthens us to move beyond pain into a greater anointing. A cross season precedes a throne season of equal proportions—the greater the cross, the greater the throne.

Maturity and authority are acquired when we embrace transformation in the midst of the pain. Desires within us and pain around us, create the needed intensity of fire to purify our motives and forge our identity. God dreams will always experience heavy anointing, devil fires and people problems. Until we can walk past the fires and the problems, we cannot possess the dream.

Focus of purpose in the midst of pain prepares our hearts for destiny. The same focus required to navigate past the pain, will be required to implement, administrate and complete destiny visions. Focus results from a thought life based in truth that naturally conquers problematic circumstances. Our destiny always increases the joy of life for others by removing or minimalizing limitations that are generally accepted.

Through the light bulb, Thomas Edison lessened the danger of fires and the unhealthy fumes created by the kerosene lamps. The light bulb was also more effective, convenient and versatile. To invent or produce a practical light bulb it took over 3,000 experiments and twelve years. Sacrifice, persistence and dedication over many years are required to create life opportunities for others. Our destiny enhances the possibilities that others can consider.

The suffering of the cross was not the focus of Jesus—we were, but the cross was the only path to us. We cannot help others without suffering personally. Time, thought, money and emotions must be invested to help others reach their purpose.

Jesus did not come to earth so He could win over the enemy, but so we could. Through the suffering of the cross and conquering death in the earth, Jesus gained the victory for those that would believe in Him. True destiny gives others victory.

A deep passion for a desired outcome presses us past our personal comfort and the intimidation of confrontation to bring the much needed change. We must not allow self-centered thinking or a survival spirit to derail destiny. Transformation in the earth is a painful process, but it is the only door to our future. It must always start on the inside of us and work out to what is around us.

Our future assignments are greater than our present identity. The power of a truck as it approaches a mountain is revealed in the lower gears as the top gear is designed for cruising. A mountain of resistance can reveal the power through our lower gears as we shift into our core identity.

Honor is a healing balm that dismantles the immobilizing grip of pain off our hearts and faith—freeing our core identity to emerge and thrive. Since pain was placed there by the enemy through people, Father God knows that it must be undone in like manner. He sends people to honor us, teach us new truths and love us back into trusting Him as they walk with us out of the shadows of death and the fear of evil—into our destiny.

Fear tells us that we will lose again if we try. Fear tries to name us a loser. Failure is a part of success that is easier to overcome if we see ourselves as a winner that must navigate through failures to obtain victory. Fear whispers that we will be hurt over and over *again*. "Again" represents the past that is now pretending and demanding to be our future. Emotional pain creates a controlling force that produces broken thinking with extremely limited possibilities.

The healing of our emotions is required to uncover the treasure of our identity that God created in us to help others reach their destiny, and ours as well. Unhealed emotions bury us in what others have done to us or our past mistakes. Healthy emotions are the breath of life that unlocks the genius God created in our identity that accelerates our destiny as we dream again and again.

Pain will alter our identity and beliefs, limiting or totally stealing our destiny if it is left unchecked. Bitterness, anger and fear mixed into a fine blend of sarcasm will imprison our thinking, spirit and core being and sabotage our destiny for the rest of our life if it is not removed.

Sarcasm is a negative attitude with an underlying critical spirit that is strangely enjoyed by those who are dying from its poison. Comedians can make a living off of thought patterns that laughs at expected failure that destroys success—leaving us with hopelessness.

Accomplishing goals of value always includes discomfort and pain. Pain is a natural part of the process in our journey to destiny, like an Olympic athlete. We must be aware there are always required sacrifices that must be embraced to enter any dream. There are also painful transitional moments required to advance a dream, but we cannot confuse growing pains with the attack of the enemy through people, situations or personal failure that tries to suffocate us—with pain. Sometimes the resistance of the enemy and our personal issues are so intertwined that it is unfruitful to try to understand it all—just increase with new thoughts and renewed hope until breakthrough occurs.

Joseph's dreams were fulfilled through a journey of favor, rejection, accusations, and an unbelievable promotion. It didn't seem like the street to success that he expected—or any of us would choose. These are not different streets to be chosen or avoided in our journey—it's the only street to our destiny. Travel any numerical major route, like Rt. 8, through a city and watch the many name changes, but it is still the same street we started on to reach our destination.

We can always dream beyond the pain we have experienced or are presently facing, if the pain does not possess our spirit and direct our thinking. Pain attempts to suffocate faith, hope and love over time. Pain restricts our creative thought process and the ability to dream. It can be difficult or even impossible to think while we are experiencing intense pain.

The enemy tries to use pain to create a judgment against God in our hearts that builds a warped relationship with Him that can never fully function. The enemy had to warp the relationship between Adam and Eve and Father God with deceptive thoughts before he could shatter their perfect destiny in His presence. Seeing Father God correctly is required to live in our "Garden of Eden," our place of purpose in His presence.

A warped view leads to sin that separates us from God as we rebel against Him and trash our identity with insecurity and unbelief. If we do not listen to our parents, that is one problem, but if I tell my parents that they are not doing a good job of raising me that is a judgment against them. That judgment creates a much deeper problem than my disobedience. Christians can repent of their sins and yet not deal with the judgments that they still have against Father God.

Pain can bring us to a fresh start as we change our ways and shift our identity or it can lock us into the past with accusations and judgments against Father God. *"Why didn't you choose me, God? I was more qualified. They failed. I would have been a better choice. Why did you bless them before me? You're not helping me with my dreams or giving me what I asked for. Do you know I am here? Do you see my situation?*

Do you really care about me at all?" These are Christian judgments against Father God that disrupt and delay the process of achieving our destiny.

Pain causes us to doubt Father God's love and favor for us in this present life. Yet, in the face of pain, Jesus displayed His undying love for us on the cross. Jesus took authority over the pain we would experience in our lives on the cross—a place of extreme physical and emotional pain.

In the midst of total rejection, laughing mockers, being falsely judged, provoking accusations, abandonment by most of His faithful followers, and verbal raging hatred by His enemies—He loved all of them past His pain. He put their actions into perspective in the midst of a cup He did not want to drink— *Father, forgive them for they don't know what they are doing.*

He requested this forgiveness for them in the midst of His agony they had inflicted. He defeated pain and the desire for revenge at the cross. We must live in what He did for us, not what others have done to us. He calls us to live past our own mistakes, by living in Him—the Victorious One.

The distrust the serpent created in Adam and Eve warped their relationship with Father God and led to their disobedience that opened the door for the enemy to spew hell into the perfect Garden of Eden that knew no pain. Jesus brought healing and hope from heaven into our Father's world to crush the pain of the serpent. Never forget, this is our Father's world—it belongs to Him.

The brothers of Jabez, like many people in life, did not get past the pain, but Jabez did. We cannot allow the multitude or close friends who choose to carry pain through life to influence us to do the same. We tend to gravitate out of concern towards those who are in emotional pain, but we cannot live there and keep a healthy outlook on life, even though they may demand it.

Prayer: *Father God, I rejoice that You chose me. You have called me and qualified me for that which You have chosen me to do. You have lifted me past my failures to my destiny. You have given me dreams and You are building in me that which I need to accomplish all that you have placed in my heart. I receive the new You are building in me. You are working beyond my understanding to open up my future. Thank you, Father God, for always being in my life—You are my life. Everything I have need of, You have provided. Your amazing favor is opening up doors that the enemy cannot shut. Your presence is carrying me into my destiny. You are my wisdom, confidence, and strength. Hallelujah!*

Identity Distortion

The enemy sends pain through events to distort who we are thus diminishing what we can do. Pain can be overwhelming, but we can't allow it to own us. Pain is designed by the enemy to distort our identity and highjack our destiny. Pain fragments our identity stunting its healthy growth.

A distorted identity undermines our value. This is huge. Our value is directly connected to our destiny. A distorted identity creates confusion into our thinking and muddles our purpose. A distorted identity demands that our value be maintained through our constant performance that must be acknowledged by others—success and insecurity often run together.

A healthy identity continues to grow and mature out of the celebration of Father God over our lives. The value we gain from Him is the foundation and source of all we do, delivering us from the need of people's fickle opinions. Destiny runs with honor.

A broken identity creates a shattered value system. We can be brilliant in moments, but find difficulty to see ourselves as brilliant. Therefore we operate from an identity of above-average, with flashes of brilliance, but that identity will never create or sustain the brilliance we were created to bring to the earth.

A total lack of identity is like an unlocked door to the bank vault filled with valuable treasures. It will be ransacked until all the treasures are stolen. It is time for us to get back the treasures that the enemy has stolen from our identity. Our Identity stores and guards the value of our life.

There are times in life we must take our identity out of the hands of a trusted person who helped us in a past season that became jealous and destructive towards us. We start with forgiveness and then wisdom to keep a healthy distance. We honor their help in the past season, but we must live in the honor of the Lord to sustain our identity to enter greater purpose.

Nothing healthy grows outside of honor—even us. The Father verbally honored Jesus before men on the earth, the angels in heaven, and Satan and his demons in hell after His baptism. The Father's honor was strategic to the battle that Jesus was about to face with Satan for forty days in the wilderness. The Father's honor launched the ministry of Jesus. No ministry or destiny is launched without honor—even Jesus.

Fathers are called to launch the ministry of the next generation with honor.

If we walk in the dishonor or negative circumstances or critical comments, instead of the honor of Father God, we are more susceptible to the attacks of the enemy. That's why the enemy tries to keep vain imaginations and dishonor in our head. We must cast them down before they slam us down.

Heaven honored Jesus before He faced the dishonor of others and the cup He did not want to drink. Sin has pleasure that sours. Obedience has delight that anoints us, our purpose, and our path. When we drink a cup of suffering out of obedience, we honor His pleasure. Some of our greatest rewards from God will come from following Him in the darkest times.

We need fathers and mothers in the Spirit or close friends who will strengthen our identity in difficult times and we must learn to do it for others. Sometimes we will need to help those who helped us journey forward in a past season. We need each other to complete our destiny journeys. A pointed word of encouragement at the right time can shift a losing battle into a victory.

A young pastor was struggling with several major issues as he was trying to breathe life back into a struggling church. There were many storms at different levels. I gave him wise advice, but the honor I gave him was more effective. I looked at him and said, "You are greater than the storm." Over a year later I was honoring him for how he had brought new life and growth to the church. He did not mention the advice I had given him, but he reminded me of the honor I spoke over him that I had almost forgotten. Honor is a boundless strength to vision.

Jacob deeply loved Rachel and his pain was great as she slipped towards death, but he refused to allow their collective pain to name their newborn baby, "son of my sorrows." He honored the Lord above that overwhelming pain he was experiencing in the moment. We cannot allow pain to name our future. Jacob watched his wife, Rachel, die as she was giving birth to their son, but Jacob named him Benjamin, "son of my right hand."

Jacob did not succumb to the pressure of pain, but enlarged his son's destiny with vision. We must never allow pain to name the future of what Father God is birthing in us, through us, for us, or around us. These are parallel dimensions of reality that affect each of us in profound ways.

The blanket of pain that covers us during great losses is also positioning us on a welcome mat in front of a door of new opportunities. We would have missed some of our greatest blessings, if our comfort and plans had not been interrupted by painful situations.

My wife had adamantly refused to go to a doctor after the cancerous growth had been detected by her doctor, a bit larger than a tennis ball. A much younger woman in our church had just died from a botched cancer stomach operation that had 97% success rate. My wife chose a radical diet and faith, over my strong objections.

She looked me in the face and said, "It's my life to live and to die the way I choose." I felt in my heart that she would not live if she did not go to the doctors immediately. The inner tsunami of emotional turmoil came to rest in His presence.

In less than six months it grew to the size of a football. The horrendous pain finally caused her to concede to go for an operation and chemotherapy. After one year she was declared cancer free of ovarian cancer. Within weeks there were signs of breast cancer that resulted from the extended wait before removing cancerous growth. In the midst of pain, the pressure was increasing.

After a regular eye exam, my doctor told me that I needed to see a specialist as there were some serious concerns he had about my vision. I went through a battery of tests weeks later. The new doctor sat me down and asked me if I had been under a heavy stress and the nature of my occupation. I felt slightly embarrassed to inform him that I was a pastor as I explained some of the stress I was facing at home. He paused with an uncomfortable silence while gazing into my face he said, "You might want to consider a change of careers as you are going blind." He explained several things about macular degeneration and a detaching retina.

I left his office stunned. I didn't know what to think. There was so much on my plate that I could not even process it. I simply said, "I cannot receive this. I will not receive this." It was a tired faith, but it was a stubborn faith. I believe that God had even given me a gift of faith. That doctor sent me to another specialist who took internal pictures of my eyes with machines I had never seen before. After she reviewed the photos and other results, she said, "Your eyes are fine. I don't see any unusual problems."

Months later when I was renewing my driver's licenses, I adjusted my glasses for my eye exam. The examiner asked me if wore my glasses when I drove. I responded that I normally did not. She asked me to remove my glasses and take the eye exam. She informed me that she was removing glasses as a requirement from my driver's licenses as I had passed it with flying colors. The rejoicing was deep in my heart, but limited in time as my wife's frailty and the fluid build-up in her lungs from the cancer was signaling the end was near.

Over her objections, I contacted her siblings to come to visit her as her days on earth were coming to an end. She did not want any "death visits" as we were still standing and believing for a miracle, but she was blessed when they came to see her. The emotional tensions were high and the pain was deep. The pain was trying to devalue my identity and worth as a husband, father, and pastor.

I chose to go into a deeper relationship with Father God, coming before His face in a way that had never done before. The pain did not cause me to grow; the pain required my choices to go deeper—deeper with God than I had ever been before.

There were other personal pressures from my one son who was living a rebellious lifestyle at the time, who could not handle watching his mother die. He and a few others felt that it was my fault and that I should have handled it differently.

Several weeks before my wife passed away with cancer after a two year battle, about forty people left the church to start another one in our area. Three couples that had worked with her came to tell her that they were leaving our church and starting a new one. The pain was intense. She turned to me, after the last couple left, and yelled in a very hurt and angry voice, "What are they trying to do to me? Kill me?"

I never expected to outlive my wife. I was fifty-five year old widower stunned with grief. It was difficult as a senior pastor to move forward with an entire congregation that was also grieving. Most people were very supportive, yet some judged me for a lack of faith or doing the right thing. I kept my eyes on Him like never before.

When God brought LuAnne into my life as a gift, some of those who wept with me were now judging me. They did not want to move from their grief that soon or maybe never. I didn't realize how much grief was still on me even as I was rejoicing on our engagement day until LuAnne leaned over and gently kissed me. I could not initiate the kiss—I was still too broken. To my surprise, I literally sensed the grief leave me as my future kissed me. Some of you need to let your future kiss you to break you out of the grief of the past season.

Pain will detain us—let's not be a prisoner of our past. Father God had "kissed me" many times throughout my recovery, but He used her kiss for a major deliverance. Father God is sending people to "kiss" you. Receive their love for you and their celebration of you, not based on what you have suffered, but rather who you are to them and Father God.

Why am I telling this story? I am not writing these truths out of a vacuum, but out of life events that the Lord has walked me through. The truths that I am sharing with you did not come from a cheap ticket and neither will yours. My stories will not save you from going through painful events, but they will encourage you that there is vision and purpose beyond the darkest of days. I actually have to choose what painful stories to include that would be helpful and which ones to leave out.

It's not that I have that many more big stories of pain, but others that were smaller in scope were huge stealth attacks against my value and purpose. We must beware of "the little foxes that spoil the vines (Song of Solomon 2:15 NKJV)." Never underestimate the effects of the smaller stealth attacks that occur in the midst of broken relationships of those close to us producing some of the most demonic accusations, whether spoken or implied, searing our hearts and our minds—sinking our dreams by shattering our value.

__Prayer:__ Lord I am asking you to reveal the devaluing and the distortion of my identity through accusations from broken relationships, whether spoken or implied, so they can be dismantled and discarded. I release myself and them from the painful prison of judgment by the blood of the Lamb and my personal forgiveness. I speak the healing grace of Jesus and His fruitful favor over all involved. I bless them and received unlimited blessings from You, Lord. Father God, I receive from you the restoration of my identity and its continual growth that advances my destiny.

I had to shatter the limitations of pain, just like everyone else. We each have our own pain that is so deep, even though the events may be different, the pain is not. He knows your pain. He knows you. He knows what He has for you—above the pain of the past. "Kiss" the joy of your future and experience a quantum shift in your identity. I advanced from a grieving widower to a rejoicing fiancé. It was a life-giving identity shift.

It is a possibility that the mother of Jabez could have been dying while birthing Jabez. Her husband also could have died after she became pregnant, since he is never mentioned. Since Joseph was not mentioned at the cross of Jesus, nor in the upper room, most scholars believe that Jesus suffered the loss of his father as a young man.

It also is not uncommon for children in the womb to be impacted by their parents' negative personal situations during the pregnancy or at the birth of the child. Jabez's mother could have experienced the loss of her father or mother during the pregnancy or even a devastating financial collapse. We must be cleansed of any pain that entered our spirit that came through our parents or surrounding environment from the moment of our conception until we were birthed so that we can freely enter all the blessings Father God has for us.

Jesus never focused on the pain He would bear on the cross— even though He had to face it in the Garden of Gethsemane. Rather He focused on the love He had for us. We were "the joy that was set before Him." The deep love we have for what we do and those who benefit from our purpose helps us endure the required sacrifices. Every godly sacrifice we endure seats us on a throne in His presence.

"Looking unto Jesus, the author and finisher of our faith, who for the joy that was set before Him endured the cross, despising the shame, and has sat down at the right hand of the throne of God Hebrews 12:2 NKJV."

Peter had to forgive himself for denying that he knew Jesus. Jesus revealed it to Peter before it happened. Jesus saw Peter beyond his failure before Peter ever experienced it. Peter was not Judas. Our Father sees us beyond our failures as well. Jesus built Peter's identity to withstand failure. Jesus built identity in Peter, and He is building identity in each of us.

Jesus referred that He was a seed that must fell into the ground—or remain alone. We were created from the earth, and we who believe and pursue Him are the "good soil" that receives the seed of "Christ" producing thirty, sixty and a hundred fold.

Father God did not save us to replace the identity He created in us. The Anointed One dwelling in us releases and empowers the purpose of our identity that He created in us.

Peter was a fisherman, and through the anointing, he became a "fisher of men." Saul was a Pharisee of Pharisees, a well-studied zealous leader who persecuted the church. When the anointing flowed through his life he became the zealous apostle who penned the majority of the New Testament, establishing church doctrine with great love and care.

He wanted to reproduce Jesus through the Body of Christ, the children of God. The identity of a seed determines the fruit it produces in the ground—us. Our identity is completed through His seed in our lives—"Christ in us, the hope of glory." This is foundational to enter the harvest that includes the "greater works" Jesus said that He would do through us. A seed can only reproduce its identity. What we are—is what we will reproduce in others—not what we have or say. The greatest revival will be seedtime and harvest. Our identity must be restored in Christ for the greatest revival coming—just like Peter.

Father God had just changed the name of Jacob to Israel. His name shifted from "a heel-grabber, one who supplants or undermines," to "a prince" with Father God. Our fallen identity must be transformed to our created identity. Only Jesus, the Son of God, was born a king. Father God spoke identity to Jacob before he entered his God vision. A God spoken identity shift is a pain breaker and a game changer. God does not need to change our names, but our identity must shift like Jacob's before we can enter our promised land. His new identity became the name of the nation.

Father God's vision for our lives is a journey embedded with honor that continues to correct our identity at strategic moments that empowers our purpose into destiny. If we stop in our journey, the honor that He prepared for us is still waiting. It will not come to us; we must continue to passionately pursue Him and His created plans for our lives to enter it.

Visions build greater value in us creating a subsequent identity shift that allows us to entertain other possibilities that we never imagined before we received the last identity shift. We are changing from glory to glory. Visions are secured with honor. We change—and then we change what is around us.

The Shame of Pain

Pain is connected to how we feel about an event. Shame is connected to how we feel about ourselves. Pain is a source that naturally creates shame if it is not brought into God's healing love and presence for revelation. Vision sees the purpose above the pain and beyond the shame we will all face in our journey to success.

Shame attacks our identity, diminishes our hope and brings depression to steal our destiny. Satan shames us, the Father celebrates us and we analyze. We must determine now who we will listen to in this next season. We must not think in darkness or the grey matter between our ears—we must think in His light. Living in Father God's love and wisdom breaks the grip of shame, repositioning our hearts in favor and shifting our expectations for the future.

The enemy uses people's words and actions to shame us, but we must agree before shame can have a place in our thinking and emotions. As we live in the loving wisdom of Father God, His truth brings honor to us that will extinguish the fiery arrows of shame the enemy launched toward us through events and people.

One night LuAnne and I took my oldest son out to a meal at a nice restaurant with his new friend that I loved, but whom I did not approve. After the meal, my son asked me to drop him off at a location near the beach where he had chosen to live homeless with his friend. As I watched them walk away from my car, emptiness started filling my heart. Then the enemy spoke to me; "You have failed as a father. What kind of a father are you?" It was a direct attack against my identity and purpose as a father in the Body of Christ.

I brought these accusations by the enemy before Father God as I was still watching him walk into the dark evening with his friend. He told me that I was a good father and that my son's decisions were his present choices, not a reflection on my fatherhood. God's thoughts entered my mind. *"I have called many and only one made all the right choices. The imperfection of My sons and daughters is not a reflection of My fatherhood, but My unending love for each of them is."* We must defeat the painful lies of the enemy with Father God's healing revelation.

Unresolved pain that moves into our emotions keeps shame alive inside our hearts. Unresolved pain can be crushed by the existing peace and trust that we have in God even before the circumstance changes. There can be no restoration maintained with shame controlling our hearts.

We may cover shame with timid fear or a loud voice, protect it by logic, deny it with outbreaks of anger, or obscure it with success. Peace and joy is the absence of shame. Shame requires our agreement to flourish. Never agree with shame. Honor and Shame speak to our identity. Confusion comes when we listen to both.

Shame demands that we control our lives to avoid more pain. Control actually isolates us from God and others. Control is a tug of war that will never win over shame. Shame expands under a spirit of control.

We must see ourselves as less than who we are for shame to take root in our thinking. The enemy tries to devalue us with shame so he can steal our future or limit our sphere and impact. If we are not healed from past hurts, it will devalue our identity. Shame can easily own any of us at any time if we have a hint of self-hatred in our hearts. Any place we wish we were created differently, it is a form of self-hatred. Celebrating who we are in the Lord creates a healthy secure identity.

Pain signals the beginning place where we have the opportunity to raise our level of resolve and commitment. Strength of vision affects our choices in hard times and charts our future, positively or negatively. If we respond incorrectly the first time, relax—we will have another opportunity to win over pain in the near future. Living above existing pain is the mark of champions.

Shame is toxic, but it still can appear as a natural part of our lives in unique aspects of our thinking that we accept as normal in our convoluted reasoning that steals portions of our destiny—often unaware to us. Hidden shame that has become a part of our identity, which we carry unknowingly, is a greater attack on our destiny than the obvious shame that we have already dismantled.

Just recently I was thinking about an event in my childhood that affected me in more ways than I realized. I was probably eleven years old. Our house was located next to the road in a rural area, so the traffic was not at a residential reduced speed. The problem was that our new German shepherd was several years old and was never trained. He would chase cars on the grass beside the road in front of the house.

I tried to think of what I should do to train him. An idea came to me that I should put a rope across his path that would trip him about twenty feet from the road. I couldn't find a rope, so I settled for a string that was about thirty feet long. I lifted the string as He ran towards the road the first time. He easily broke through it to my shock. Instead of turning and running alongside of the road as he always did, he ran into the highway area and was struck by the delivery truck—killed right in front of my eyes.

I can't even express all the grief and sense of failure that hit me as I looked at my new dog lying dead in the road. It only hit me several weeks ago the spirit of failure and hopelessness the enemy put over my heart through that event that marinated my identity as a failure that would have marginal success. The lie whispered; "Dale, you really can't change anything. Your plans will never work or help others. You will only create more problems." Failure and hopelessness is based in shame.

Shame has a voice. Shame is very deceiving. We naturally compensate the effects of shame to survive. There is no amount of success that can remove shame from our identity—it takes God's healing love and truth. The defensive grid we create in our spirit and mind to protect us, will ultimately suppress our true genius, steal our faith and downsize our vision.

In this defensive grid we blame others and the circumstances, but we secretly judge ourselves. Shame moves us into fear and marks us as a failure. Life is unsafe and people are hurtful. Fear forces us to take control to avoid pain. Fear can cause us to quit. We might continue to work, but we have quit loving or believing—we become the walking dead. When we hit that place, we need to cry out like Jabez. It births life—like a newborn baby's cry.

Keep asking the Holy Spirit to reveal any events, especially from your childhood, that made you feel less than others. Where it made you feel less than, is where Father God wants to set you free. There is a new inside of you that you have never met.

Shame is a greater enemy of vision than unbelief. Shame is rooted in our identity. Unbelief is our view towards our ability and God's. Shame is my view of me. If I am wrong, everything I do is wrong. Shame must be shattered before we can dream with heaven about our lives—our destiny.

If someone yelled at us and called us stupid it is very hurtful, but we normally will push back that obvious attack. When we failed a test and thought we were stupid—that is a stealth shame attack. It was an internal assessment by our quiet inner voice that lowered our value and limited our genius. We are often totally unaware of the depth of that shame, but it is deadly to our destiny.

My history teacher in 7th grade gave us a pop quiz the second week of a new school. I flunked it as I had not read the homework assignment. The pain that came over me when he said in front of the class, "You may be a Mast, but you are certainly not like your sister!" made me forget that I became one of his favorite students with "A" grades in his class.

Shame can actually blind us to the strengths we have and the victories we have achieved. It always focuses us on our failures and weaknesses—loudly.

A bank executive can focus on the fact that he was never talented enough to make the basketball team in high school, or he can think about the financial strategy he created that funded the new college sports program with improved sport facilities, hiring the high school coach on his advice that created a winning season his first year of coaching, that drew better players which created a NCAA basketball championship team in five years.

The hurt of being cut from the team in high school cannot be masked by becoming the owner of an NBA championship team. He must embrace his identity as a gift to others. His desire to be on the basketball team was a desire that would become an assignment, but it was not his identity. He was not a basketball player, but a builder of an NCAA championship team.

If any of us focus on the negative parts of our lives, or simply listen to the quiet whispers from them, we see ourselves incorrectly and never sign up for the right assignments that God created us to do. Little lies can make a huge difference in the way we approach our destiny. Lose the lies. Train in truth.

After three years of a miracle ministry, amazing love and teachings with great authority, Jesus appeared to over five hundred people. Only one hundred and twenty believers were waiting in the upper room when the Holy Spirit came.

Jesus did not look like a success to the untrained eye in that moment—only one hundred and twenty people after three years of ministry? There are many larger churches today gathered in one year. Jesus could have looked down from heaven as the Holy Spirit empowered the one hundred and twenty believers wondering if He really made a difference. "Where are the five thousand I fed?"

We desire large fruit stands, God deals in seeds. Seeds are heaven's wisdom and strategy that create orchards. Humility plants small seeds that produce the harvest of heaven. Value the small seeds. Plant them. Water them. Weed them. Wait for them. Don't leave the field you've planted, the harvest never fails. Shame has a flight pattern that leaves before the harvest or plows up what was planted.

Father God honored Jacob as a prince to Him, making Jacob a prince to others. Honor is a shame breaker. Israel is an identity shift that produced an assignment shift for Jacob. It was not just about Jacob's identity, it was about the twelve tribes that would become Israel.

The future of the earth hinges on our identity. Jerusalem is the capital of Israel. Jerusalem is not the capital of Jacob. Israel is the dream of God and his grandfather, Abraham. God dreams are accessed through identity shifts.

Pain had been removed from Jacob's identity and name by Father God giving him a new name. Now the "Israel" in Jacob was removing it from his newly born son whom his dying wife named from her pain. These two events both occurred in the same chapter, Genesis 35 sequentially.

In Father God's kingdom, the princes He honors with a new identity are called to give honor to the identity of others. If we see someone who never gives honor, we know they have never received honor—even if it was given to them by others. Honor must be received and treasured—it is a basic requirement to truly become an honor donor.

It is critical we learn how to receive honor. We must meditate on the words of honor that were given to us and let it remove other words of dishonor that were burned into our identity. Repeat the words of honor until it lifts out and removes any strongholds dishonor created. Then we must allow those truths of honor to hunt down every lie that we have accepted in our life. Ask the Holy Spirit to expose the lies that we have accepted as truth. It is an amazing journey of freedom.

There is a deceiving critical spirit in shame that tries to warp the identity of all of us. We might respond faithfully to God when someone dishonors us—even blessing them, but it did not lessen the fact that it degraded our value and warped our identity. It is easier to repent of the anger we have towards someone who shamed us, than to discern how that shame warped our identity.

The enemy uses shame to attack us in different ways. Anger, hopelessness or unforgiveness lessens the anointing on our lives. The enemy will also steal or lessen what God is anointing—our identity. Many Christians correct their attitudes to be like Jesus, but overlook the identity Jesus lived from—"My Son, in whom I delight." We must sense His delight in us. It brings wholeness to our identity.

Giving honor increases our capacity to receive greater honor. We receive honor in direct proportions to the way we give honor to others. We can only reap what we sow. Giving honor to those who have dishonored us opens the gates of honor to flood us. Honor is always based in truth that releases freedom. Flattery is exaggerations that attempts to plant pride and fear in our hearts, giving the flatterer control over us.

A painful name was given to Jacob by his mother due to his wrestling with his brother in her womb and at his birthing. It is interesting that Jacob experienced his identity shift wrestling with God as he was preparing to face his brother. Unless we wrestle with the right one, we cannot shift our identity to match our promised destiny. Jacob wrestled with God, not his twin brother, as he faced the pain of his past that had come to destroy him. Jacob was seeking God for his life, but God wanted to give him a new identity for his life.

Just as God changed the name of Jacob to Israel, it gave him the ability to do the same for his son Benjamin. Until the pain is removed from our identity, we cannot help others. These issues affect nations and history.

We can bring comfort to others as we listen to their story and validate their pain connected to the events as we share similar events from our lives. Comfort and healing are two different entities, even though they are companions. Comfort for a dying patient is very different from healing for a dying patient.

Listening brings comfort to the brokenhearted, because pain in relationships always involves bad communication. We cannot walk anyone in pain much beyond our point of progress in our journey to healing. Our healing journey is accelerated as we help others find truth that releases healing. Pain comes through people, healing comes through people.

Pain comes through life, but we can't let it name us. The birthing struggle with his older brother named him Jacob. The pain of this struggle increased as Jacob bought Esau's birthright and then lied to his father causing him to flee his twin brother, Esau, who comforted himself with the thought of killing Jacob.

More pain entered Jacob's life as he had to flee Laban, his father-in-law. Laban told Jacob it was in his power to hurt him, but God had warned him not even to speak "good or bad" to Jacob. Good words can manipulate people, bad words bring damage. Father God did not want Laban to alter Jacob's path from his destiny through his "good or bad" words. What words have changed our path? We are often unaware how our Father protects us at vulnerable transition times. He looked out for Jacob and He is looking out for us.

It was crucial that Jacob's identity as a prince was established, giving him authority to diffuse the pain that existed between him and Esau. Father God wanted Jacob to see his life in relationship to Him as a prince before he met Esau. Jacob could not succeed as a "heel-grabber" in this confrontation. Identity upgrades are required to navigate through broken relationships.

Prayer: *Holy Spirit, reveal any events to me, especially from my childhood, that made me feel less than others. Where it devalued me, I am asking that you would set me free from the negative judgments against myself. I break all judgments that I have received against my identity and purpose. Father, I repent where I have believed other voices, even my own, over my life instead of yours. Father God, please reveal the value and purpose I have to You and those you have placed in my life. I rejoice in You as You sing songs of deliverance over me.*

Chapter Three

HONOR SHATTERS SHAME

Painful events have a natural devaluing impact to our identity. Each time pain attaches to our lives it attempts to remove honor. Honor, conversely, removes pain. Honor is love based. We cannot honor someone we hate, but we could give them an award for what they accomplished. Clearly those are two different issues.

When we honor Father God for the gift He has placed in us, it releases the anointing and the purpose of that gift. When we honor the Lord for how He has created us, it releases the genius and destiny He placed in us.

If a gold bar is taken from a treasure chest put in a paper bag it does not lose any value. It simply would be a surprise to anyone who opened the bag. If it is thrown into filthy garbage dumpster it does not lose any value, but anyone one finding it would immediately remove it, clean it and place it in a protected place of honor. The enemy often tries to hide our value in the garbage of life, but the Father will send people to elevate us.

Father God has created us out of His glory, in His likeness and image, by His genius so that we could function as His sons and daughters. We are a treasure to Him—and *God so loves the world*. He seeks us out to allow the life of Jesus Christ to flow through each of us in a very unique way. He places angels around us to protect what He treasures. Just as we have plans for our treasures, so does He—that's you and me.

If a gold bar is placed among diamonds and other gold jewelry, the value of the Gold is not increased; it has simply been placed in a correct environment. Somedays you may feel like you are living in a treasure chest and other days in a ripped brown paper bag. Someone may have thrown you in the dumpster, but you are still gold to God.

We must draw on the value of who we are to Him, not what surrounds us. The value of our purpose is measured by the cost of the anointing He has placed over our lives. How we feel about ourselves on a given day or during a tough season does not determine our value, but it might limit our purpose. It is critical that we honor who He has made us when we do not feel valuable. What we do when we are struggling to see our value determines our next season. We are to choose to live out of our known value with purpose and thankfulness. Then the attempts of the enemy to devalue us actually become the stepping stones to the next level.

Miracles, signs and wonders come from honor. We need the touch of heaven to be healthy and whole—breaking the hellish thoughts and emotions that try to bind us or block us. The enemy tries to make us feel like garbage so we will settle for the dumpster life, but Father God lovingly embraces us as His treasure. Live a treasured life to honor Him.

When we honor how the Lord has made us, it unlocks our unique treasure and the genius to operate in it. Learn from others, mature and grow — but be yourself. God designed each of us uniquely for a purpose — right down to our fingerprints. The original painting has the greatest value, not the reprints. Cancel your desire to be a reprint of someone famous, it cheapens your value.

Value was not put on the life of Jabez at his birth, but rather he was devalued by the pain of his mother experienced. She transferred it to his identity. As much as any mother loves a new-born baby, intense pain can devalue what would they normally embrace and highly value. We must guard our words and actions around people when we are the midst of intense pain, so that we do not devalue others. Jesus valued the people that caused His pain at the cross.

The enemy knows that pain we experience in our childhood and especially within our family will affect every relationship for the rest of our lives unless we break free of the life patterns that pain creates. If we live feeling devalued, we will even transfer it to those we love the most. We will not love them for who they are, but rather what they do for us because of insecurities.

We do not know what pain entered the life of Jabez, but his prayer reveals it was present. Jabez rose up above his pain and made a choice. We always have a choice available to us that empowers us to enter into a new season of peace, blessing and joy.

Pain that creates strongholds in our minds is not the result of one event, even though it is very important to know where it started. Strongholds come from a series of events that affect our belief system in a particular area of life. We might easily believe that we can prosper because of past successes, but we could also believe that we will always be alone and rejected because of repeating negative experiences.

It is normal to deny our need for help because of our success. Jabez rose above the pain in his life therefore he was more honorable than his brothers. I believe the actual birthing pain of Jabez was compounded by another devastating event in his mother's life. God designed blessings to come through our family. The enemy knows this principle and tries to intercept our blessing with traumatic experiences within our family.

When I was thirty my father asked me if I was ready to be the pastor of the three year old church that he had pioneered. I was the assistant pastor at that time and felt the call to the ministry. Every year there was a church split. I was shocked by the first one, but started thinking that it was normal after the second one. It created a view of pastoring that was making me tentative about my ability to deal with these problems.

My father said that we would wait to hear from our speaker at our upcoming conference in two weeks. My father asked him if God had spoken to him about the church. He seemed quite uncomfortable as he nodded his head. Steve Rathod shared that God had given him a dream. In the dream I was the pastor and my father was the assistant. Steve told God he would not even speak of it unless my father specifically asked him.

Later in the year I was set in as the pastor. The church doubled in the next six months. My father later confessed to me in the middle of a nervous breakdown that he had become jealous of me. Everything my father ever touched succeeded as a businessman. He was very effective in ministry and a natural leader.

He told me that he never really wanted to be a pastor, but others pushed him forward because of his natural leadership skills.

My father preached once a month after I became pastor. His last sermon contained a story which ended with a pointed conclusion. It really upset one man. I asked my father to talk with him about it. When I told my Dad what the man had said, my dad said that he never meant that. My mother chimed in, "Larry, you said it." My father stood to his feet said defensively, "If he (the church member) is that mad, then it must be true." He walked out of the office leaving my mother and I starring at each other.

I didn't care so much about the point of controversy as his unwillingness to talk with the man. I stopped using my father to preach as he felt unsafe to me. He felt judged and rejected. He started telling people that they should leave the church because God was not moving there anymore. The church was shattered, and half of the members left the church.

My father had been such a healing balm to the abuse my wife had suffered from her father. The honor she had for my father became a double devastation to her. She would cry each Sunday morning as we headed for church, sometimes literally shaking, only to dry her tears in the parking lot before leading worship. I was very aware that she was on the verge of a nervous breakdown.

I told my father it was his decision to make. If he wanted the church back, I would give it to him and move to my wife's hometown. He said that's what he decided. My wife and I drove to church happy for the first time in months as we looked forward to resigning that Sunday and to be moving out of the storm and into something new.

I had a great sermon planned on God's three supreme edits: I will pour out My Spirit, I will build my church, and I will return. I am resigning as pastor, but His church shall grow with my father returning as the pastor.

Ten minutes before the church service started, my Dad called. He said, "We have changed our mind. We'll keep the church (building), you keep the people." I instantly started weeping. "God, you would not do this to me?" My question was wrong, but His answer was right.

There was a "stay" in His silence that was unmistakable, but He wanted me to choose it. This was more about our relationship than the circumstances. He was building me—in the midst of everything that was falling apart—and God knew it would be crucial for my destiny. I couldn't see it, but I could see Him.

The Lord spoke to me to buy land for our future building in the midst of my tears. With fifty dollars and a word from God we purchased 42 acres just outside the city limits. Our greatest blessings are often in the middle of our greatest trials when we respond to Him and not the event.

Our church continued to grow again. My father moved away, but two years later he asked for the church building, so he could start his church again. We moved less than one mile away. The Sunday we left, he held his first service. After two years he turned the church over to my Brother-in-law and then several years later my brother became the pastor.

There had been much healing in my heart, but the pain was deep. About a decade later I asked the Lord, "What is the key to bringing this pain to an end?" He astounded me when he said, "Honor him." "But Lord, you see all the pain my Dad has caused me and my family." I replied.

As I was contemplating what to say to honor my father, I knew I could not stretch the truth. Honor is always built with truth, flattery is built with lies. I picked up the phone and called my father. The words I spoke to him I will never forget. "Dad, I honor you. You have taught me more about ministry than anyone else. But most of all, you taught me to love God and to love people. If it was not for your example in my life I would not be who I am today. I just wanted to honor you."

From that day forward, my Dad honored my ministry to others—and the Lord made sure that I heard it from several people. He never honored me to my face until I was engaged to LuAnne, twenty five years from the original devastation. Then he openly blessed me and LuAnne and the ministry God had given us several times with me present with the entire family and shortly before he died. It was a special gift.

My mother died never hearing me preach again after that split, even though she would attend our church conferences to hear guest speakers. My Dad visited my church after my mother died several times to hear me speak to my surprise.

My anointing continued to increase and the influence of my leadership expanded. Honoring others unlocks us to live in a greater honor before the Lord. If we say we love people, but do not honor them it is actually a begrudging tolerance, not true love.

Why did I put this story in this book? Each of you could tell me a story of your pain. The people and details are probably different, but the pain is the same. I did not write this book from gathered information, but from the insight that I gained from God as I struggled with my value and identity. He changed me while concurrently changing everything around me.

These are not just scriptural theories, but rather scriptural truths applied to real life situations. In the natural eye, why should any of us honor someone who has hurt us? To live above the pain, requires God's truth. Honor shatters the limitations of pain. Honor is the fruit of true forgiveness. Honor is the result of identity healing. Honor has open access to heaven. Honor releases our genius to create and our hearts to dream visions with heaven.

Pain is confusing as well as deceiving. Pain contains illogical elements when it invades our life through those we trusted that can push us to the edge of a mental collapse. Yet the pain that devastated our lives will result in great strength and compassion if we choose to release forgiveness and receive healing. It can also bring great destruction if we choose to allow the bitterness and anger from the pain to shape our thinking and spirit—sabotaging our identity and destiny.

Pain does not produce an outcome, but our choices do. Our response to pain unveils what's in our hearts—it does not create our heart. We still have a choice after a negative reaction. A negative response by a kind person will eventually create a resentful heart if it remains unchallenged by truth and unchanged by forgiveness. Choices of repentance and forgiveness can birth life and love in a death row convict. We are never beyond help or hindrance with our choices.

It is easier to see and challenge other people's attitudes than our own, but less fruitful. Negative attitudes know how to hide from the light of revelation that abides in us through Jesus Christ by distracting and deceiving us with self-pity, justification, self-righteousness, accusations and disruptive emotions blocking our ability to see the way of escape He always provides.

We cannot shift our future if we are living in the pain of the past. Pain tries to destroy or freeze our identity in the last season to keep us from evolving and maturing into the new identity required for the next season. My focus on the *what* is stealing my focus from the *who*. Our key advancement is about our new *who*, not our new *what*. Our identity is more key than our opportunities, even though they are synchronized.

We must deal with the pain of the past before we can be fruitful to our full potential in our next level. The favor of honor is required to release our future. Pain and favor can only coexist for a short time. Pain will remove the expectation of favor. Favor and faith will shield us from the demonic spirits and negative thoughts that are released from painful memories. This freedom gives us the ability to expect wonderful things for our destiny and future.

The pain of the past guards the gates to our future. Until we conquer the pain, we will not have access to what is promised. David moved past the critical judgement of his oldest brother, the doubts of the king, and the insults of Goliath to advance on the way to being king of Israel.

Father God wants us more than He wants our future. His value of us is greater than what we do for Him, but our value sets our assignments. Father God gave Jacob a God encounter to remove the pain from Jacob's identity. Father God shifted Jacob's identity from what he had done in the past, to position Jacob's identity for what He was about to do through him in the future—Israel.

Pain brings the fear of rejection and abandonment into our most important relationships. The relationship that should have been his greatest support was now his greatest fear. Father God needed to bring the pain of Jacob's broken relationship with Esau to an end so Jacob could dream with Father God.

God dreams cause us to think differently about our destiny, but a God encounter activates it. Until we dream solutions with our eyes wide open, our identity is not fully recovered nor are we established in our purpose. I have woke up from dreams thinking with God. Our dreaming equals God's thinking.

We access our God dreams through our worship and faith. Often there is more than one key that will open a given door. Everyone exalts the one that worked for them. He has many key patterns such as prayer, faith, declarations, wisdom and His Word, but they all inevitably intersect with our relationship with Him—our identity as His child.

Honor was the observable difference that set Jabez apart from all of his brothers. It was not his strength, nor his wisdom or his talents that set him apart from his brothers. That fact that he lived a more honorable life does not imply that he attained greater wealth than his brothers, but it does point to the truth that his life influenced more people. Honor influences the magnificence of the future just as much as dishonor has influenced the foulest times in history.

God is faithful to deliver us as we follow Him. Jabez knew that only God could change the pain in his life. He did not look to those dwelling in the earth for that change, but the One in heaven who is pleased to dwell with those who seek Him. Ultimately, we must all honor God like Jabez did. Jabez placed all of his future advancement in Him. Let's pray like Jabez.

Prayer: *Father God, by the blood of Jesus Christ, I renounce the spirit of shame the enemy has brought against my life. You have created me for greatness and saved me to make it possible. I thank you for the honor you have placed on my life that confronts and removes every thought of shame that tells me I am not good enough for greatness in Your Kingdom on Your earth. I will carry Your honor in my identity so that I can bring you glory in the earth. I ask that my life would reveal You to others.*

Identity Shift Breakthrough

Father God shifted Jacob's identity from a heel grabber to a prince so he could approach Esau from the strength of his new identity. Jacob had wrestled with his twin brother in his mother's womb, but now he is wrestling with God to enter that which was spoken to his mother by God.

Wrestling with God is the key to prophetic breakthroughs. We will not advance by wrestling with "brothers" who have judgments against us. If we trust our ability to change key situations concerning our future, we become our own god. Wrestle with the Changer, not those we want to change.

Jacob's identity shift positioned him to break through the pain of the past that he helped create over twenty years ago with his twin brother. That fresh encounter with Father God shifted Jacob's identity in the midst of a troubled night that opened a new day into his destiny journey that impacted the earth forever. One encounter with God can change the history of earth—let's not miss ours. They are more abundant in our worst times.

Deep troubling in our hearts creates a unique atmosphere in which we are positioned to find God, ourselves and a new faith for the future. Peripheral issues are cast aside as we focus on God and destiny. The troubling of Jabez's heart produced the depth of his cry to God that was essential for his breakthrough.

Our relationship with Father God is the key to bringing healing to every relationship and unresolved issues. He approaches us with love, mercy, faith and truth. Then He honors us with the life sacrifice of His Son so that we would love Him with everything we are. When His life moves through us, it shatters the limitations pain has created in our identity and thus our life perspective.

Our Father sowed into us the attitudes He desires from us. He displayed a model of life with keys of love and forgiveness that work in very difficult situations. If we chose to live in bitterness and unforgiveness, we will be tormented and live a diminished destiny. If we refuse to dream with God we could get stuck in success, instead of purpose.

Jacob sent gifts of love to his brother. Jacob blessed Esau. His blessings shattered the curse of pain dismantling Esau's desire for revenge—even murder. Blessings disrupt the spirit of anger. Blessings motivated by love are life changing, otherwise it is calculated manipulation. Giving to others—to get what we want is self-centered and the world has confused it with love.

Blessing others forces us to release the last remnants of our accusations against them breaking the power of the enemy to control that relationship or us. The accuser can control us through our accusations of others or ourselves—it's his territory. He is the accuser, Father God is the one who blesses. Blessing others invites Our Father to bring His miracles into that broken relationship. As we bless others, Father God displaces the enemy from our destiny with His blessings.

Jacob did not come before Esau with the birthright and the blessings it had gathered him for vindication, but he humbled himself before Esau and honored him. It is difficult to keep a spirit of anger towards someone who honors us. We cannot truly humble ourselves unless we live in His honor. We love Him because He first loved us.

A non-honored life cannot risk humility nor operate out of love. A restored life exists in honor that empowers anyone to live boldly. When we are broken we cannot see any difference between humility and humiliation as we are blinded by pride and insecurity—both are all about us. Humility factors God as the total source of our life and abilities, building authority into our purpose that is literally unstoppable.

Humiliation is the devil's attempt to destroy our value by crushing our identity so that he can steal our destiny assignments. Jabez literally moved from the pain of humiliation to healing honor by the elements contained in his prayer. Look at it again and think about it.

There was a man named Jabez who was more honorable than any of his brothers. His mother named him Jabez because his birth had been so painful. He was the one who prayed to the God of Israel, "Oh, that you would bless me and expand my territory! Please be with me in all that I do, and keep me from all trouble and pain!" And God granted him his request. 1 Chronicles 4:9, 10 New Living Translation

Humility is our heart response of worship to the honor Father God has placed on us—that provokes Him to continue exalting us to higher levels. If we gaze too long at the new place of honor He has established for us, He must step the honor back down one notch or two to keep us from idolatry.

If someone speaks ill of us, we should find a place to honor them. Defending our honor is a contradiction of truths. We would actually be defending ourselves while bringing death to someone else. Father God honored us by creating us in His image and likeness. He increases the honor on our lives as we honor Him. When we love the least among us, we honor Him. God said He would honor those who honored Him.

> *But now the LORD says: 'Far be it from Me; for those who honor Me I will honor, and those who despise Me shall be lightly esteemed. 1 Sam 2:30 NKJV*

Father God is so holy and good that He lightly esteems those who despise Him. That is simply unbelievable. He has called us to live from His glorious patterns so His power in us changes the world He died for, rather than our ungodly response to negative circumstances changing us into something He has to work around. Lucifer was called to lead all the angels in worship to Father God in the throne room, but he ended up leading a rebellion against Him. The greatness of our call is not the guarantee of our success, but our heart to honor Him is.

Only Jesus deserves all honor, because He alone is perfect in every area. If we do not honor him, we cannot truly honor anyone. We must discern the honor the Lord has placed on a person's life to truly honor them. Our honor of Father God is worship and covenant. Our honor of others is a celebration of giving thanks to Father God for them, creating unity. Apostle Paul didn't just thank Father God privately for his friends. He wrote his thanks for them in the letters that others would read as well—Godly honor is known honor.

Confetti falling on the new championship team is fake honor. Cities brace for acts of violence and destruction of property if their team wins—fake celebrations thrown by those who do not worship Him. Many will become drunk, fight with fans from their team and cursing as they attempt to enter into the honor of victory through the dark side with blaring songs of self-honor—"We are the champions...no time for losers."

Untruthful honor is flattery that releases destructive pride and destructive actions. True honor from others dismantles the dishonor the enemy attempts through others and strengthens our hearts in God. We must discern as spiritual fathers that one of our greatest assignments is to truly honor others. Honor unlocks identity, advancing purpose.

Honor is not flattery, but rather truth spoken in love that is embedded with healing to wounded emotions. When we honor people that dishonor us, it disrupts the demonic strategy. Dishonor feeds on the emotional responses based in insecurity or pride of those attacked, as it is the core spirit of the attacker. Things can go nuclear quickly, when we respond to an attacker with the same spirit of dishonor.

Confrontation of what they have done does not bring change if there is not some honor of who they are. Dishonor of who they are aligns us with the destroyer. We must know the difference if we desire to impact the earth with heaven. If we

are not living in His honor, the undertone of every confrontation will be dishonor. Our wisest efforts cannot cover the lack
of honor. A plastic smile is not life, but the love that exists in
honor is. In a plastic world, everyone knows plastic. Love is
breath-taking.

Honor is the constant flow of His presence in our lives,
not a dusty trophy. Therefore we refill our lives with honor as
we worship Him and receive from Him as our Father. Until
we know Him—His heart and His wisdom—we cannot bring
honor into confrontation.

Honor elevates the identity of whose ideas and participation
are needed to bring and sustain change. Dishonor devalues and
creates a defensive spirit for our identity survival versus the
success of our purpose. When we operate with honor, vision,
and wisdom, we will create an atmosphere that empowers the
team to bring the needed change and advancement of the vision
purpose. When a vision perishes, so do the people. Building
honor creates the needed atmosphere required for visions to be
birthed and expanded.

Jesus honored us with His love and total sacrifice, so we
chose to love and honor Him with our lives sacrificially. If we
are upset by the lack of honor others give us, we must re-center
ourselves in the foundation of honor we have received from
God. Then we must chose to set up another level of honor
for them. Their response will be a gauge to the future of that
relationship.

Not everyone we help is in our future. What God asks us to
do for the least will determine our ability to rub shoulders with
the greatest. Neither response can be based on needs. Other's

continual need for help or our driving need for importance are both deadly traps. Live from seeds, not needs.

Our ultimate source of honor must come from Father God alone, but He will send others to complete His honor over us. Jesus grew in favor with God and man. Father God increased His favor over Jesus through men. As the disciples left everything to follow Jesus, that honored Him. When people walk out of our lives we feel—dishonored.

We must also acknowledge that pigs are not impressed with pearls, so we must not waste them. We are not calling anyone a pig, but if they continue to trample our pearls we should move on into destiny as they are not a part of it. Bitterness is a tormented spirit that cannot wear pearls of honor—nor can it honor anyone else. It is often enraged when others are honored. Bitterness is a judgement against Father God, the source of honor.

Bitterness is toxic as well as a communicable disease. Bitterness provides interesting dishonoring conversations of others that removes honor from our anointing and purpose. Phone calls from others can lessen the call of God in our lives or increase it. Know when to hang out and when to hang up until our spirit is adjusted. Sometimes we are the problem, creating a greater problem.

The healing that occurred between Jacob and Esau allowed them to bury their father peacefully together. It does not appear it was the Father's will that they should live together, but it was His will for them to bless each other.

The birthright carried an understanding of blessing toward others in the family. Even though Jacob "stole" the birthright from Esau based on the word of the Lord to their mother and her scheme, it was his duty to bless Esau. The double portion birthright was given to the eldest male to watch over the needs of his siblings from the extra portion when the father was no longer alive.

Being the first-born required a father's heart towards the rest of their siblings. Christians are called church of the first-born. Our Father God desires that we would have a "father's heart" towards the rest of the family.

While Esau did not have an apparent need, Jacob was showing Esau his heart concern and care. Remember, they were twins. There was much competition between these brothers for their parents' attention. The honor Jacob gave to Esau brought him to tears and to healing.

In blessing Esau, Jacob carried the nature and heart of Father God. It kept the blessing that was on his Grandfather, Abraham and his father Isaac on the nation Israel. In reality, Israel came into being through Jacob's identity shift from heaven.

Jesus could not return to earth to reign from Jerusalem in the land of "*Jacob*." Jesus, the "*prince of peace*," will rule in the land named, "prince with God," for *a thousand years*. The shift Father God brought to Jacob affected a piece of land in the Middle East that has impacted the history of the earth forever. It happened because Father God shifted Jacob to Israel. Until a man's identity is shifted by heaven, he cannot shift the earth.

People in the earth may still see us as a "Jacob" but Father God calls us His Israel—a "prince." Father God named Jacob by His promise, not by Jacob's pain from the journey. We must see our lives from our Father's perspective, not from our past or other people's opinions. Our negative opinions of ourselves are the greatest destiny limiters.

All of our unnecessary problems in life stem from not treating others the way Father God has treated us. Satan is the root to every problem we face, because he is a liar and a thief. Jesus faced many problems that teach us how to gain the victory over the enemy in a myriad of situations.

It is interesting that Jesus was called "A man of sorrows" in Isaiah 53. The word sorrows means pains. Now look at this verse to gain greater insight.

Surely He has borne our griefs (sickness) and carried our sorrows (pains). Is 53:4 NKJV

Jesus was never sick a day in his life, yet He bore our sickness at the cross. He was anointed with joy above his brethren, yet He carried our pain at the cross. Unresolved grief and anxiety leads to physical sickness. We need to receive His joy and healing at the cross—and carry it in this present life to see our identity clearly.

If we do not see ourselves as celebrated sons and daughters of Father God, we will approach broken relationships incorrectly because we are still living from a broken identity. Our identity and value to Father God must be established within us. Our level of health most often determines the level of healing that flows through us to others.

Often the goal of confrontational meetings is centered on us being valued by others, revealing our lack of healing. Neither has completed their journey of being established in their value. Reconciliation is improbable from both sides outside of mercy of God, which I always trust.

It is difficult for any of us in broken relationships to receive value in our broken places and improbable that we will give honor without being honored first. Jesus honored us before we ever even thought of honoring Him. Let His honor shift our identity to the tipping point where we live a life that honors God and restores honor to people.

The Idol of Pity

The pain in the life of Jabez and his brothers was known during his life, yet it was hidden from our eyes. Why? Somehow many of us feel as if we have endured the most difficult painful situations in life. We arrive at these conclusions through comparisons. Several times people have voiced this opinion to me. Although most of us never will tell others, it is not unusual to believe that we have suffered more than others. Our pain is very real to us.

At first I was unsure the reasoning or purpose behind anyone adamantly voicing this statement. As I reflected over the assertive claims, several things became clearer to me. There is a value and empathy given to those that suffer. Also less is expected of those who are in pain.

Our pain is so real that it is hard to see that others have experienced the same pain in different ways. More or less is not the real issue. When we say that we have experienced more pain than others we subconsciously may conclude that Father God was unfair to us or we deserve a larger trophy. We also may be saying that we are stronger than others because we overcame greater obstacles. Either He is the strength of our hearts and portion forever—or it's all about us.

The first thought implies that He is not a good Father. The second one hints at the fact that we deserve martyr or saint status. Pride in the pain we have endured is very real. It points to our goodness and strength to endure versus His goodness and His strength in us. Pride is about us and we take the glory. Honor is about Him in our lives and we give Him the glory.

If we have had it worse than others in our minds, then we have a reason to be stuck in life. "Nobody has had it as bad as me." What are we implying? No one could ever know how we feel, so therefore no one can help us. There is no solution for the pain we face. We are now the perfect victims—beyond criticism, challenge or change—deserving eternal pity.

Therefore we cannot be held responsible for the results of our lives or our future. The pain we experienced is now an excuse for anything in us or around us—especially in that arena. We also have the right to refuse all comfort from those who care, but the comforters are not allowed to have similar, equal or greater pain—nor can they stop comforting us. Victim is an identity that lost its grip at the cross.

Pain can seem to make us the center of attention more than our accomplishments. Yet there is no reason to continue living under pain by choice, unless pity is the true goal and the seemingly safe haven of irresponsibility. Pity poisons our spirit, short-circuits our thinking and highjacks our destiny.

Pity can feel like love, but it is not. Compassion is the godly dimension. Pity is a sympathetic sorrow for one suffering, distressed or unhappy; Compassion is the sympathetic consciousness of others' distress together with a desire to alleviate it according to Merriam-Webster Dictionary. Pity can move to compassion, but pity, by definition, does not seek change.

Pity can be addictive. Pity is instant form of attention and love that all of us can be tempted to access in crises. We desire for others to tell us we that we have a right to our negative attitudes and bad choices because of the negative situation or hurtful relationship we are facing. The goal of pure pity is not freedom, but mandatory unending emotional responsiveness. Advice is resented and resisted. Advice implies that they could move on in life if they would do something different. Personal responsibility is the enemy of pity.

If the problem was removed or solved, those passing by would no longer give us their attention. If we fear not being loved, attention is a great substitute. In the final analysis, pity leaves us empty. Only love can fill our hearts, pity never will.

Pain, by its very nature, demands attention and conversation. So does Father God. The first commandment clearly states; Thou shalt have no other gods before Me. Our Father knows if He is in the first position of our lives, the idol of pain cannot reduce us to slaves of fear, bitterness and hopelessness. If we put our *"me"* above of His Me, we have entered idolatry.

Receiving His love is healing and freeing. Our love for Him and others is the first way we break the stronghold of pity. Pity is selfish, love isn't. Love others and set yourself free. Resentment is a personal prison. Hatred is a spirit of death. Love is the breath of life that delivers hope and vision.

The enemy tries to exalt the pain and the pity above the healing and love our Father God provides creating a stronghold over our lives. Then an idol of *"me"* becomes the central focus of all our conversations. The enemy tries to make pain a controlling force over our spirit, our thought process and our very being.

Pity attempts to exalt our pain above God. Lucifer was cast out of heaven when he tried to exalt himself above God. If we exalt our pain above God and His help, we cast ourselves into a place where hell has the advantage over us.

God's love is always reaching out to us through Jesus, but we must receive Him and His thoughts about our circumstances. As Christians we can receive salvation from Jesus, but deny Him access to our problems as we retain control. Problems have the opportunity to work out of us that which never works— so He can work through us.

Another way to break the controlling force of pain is by praising Him. Our thankfulness concerning our life is also another dimension of this truth. Praise is a force that exalts our Father above the pain. Our strength increases in praise, but it takes a determined choice to praise Him in the midst of pain. The praise of Paul in Silas after being beaten and chained, broke the chains of every prisoner and opened the doors of the jail. In the worst times, our praise will produce the most amazing results.

We can actually live our lives focused on past pain. It would be the same as driving a car with our view of the road in front of us as small as a rearview mirror—with the rest of our normal windshield becoming a mirror as we continue to focus on ourselves and the pain in the past. Our future will be a perilous journey into deeper pain because we have traded a vision of hope for the painful memories of the past.

We become more committed to what we want to avoid versus where we are going. It creates an impracticable vision for our life, blocking our ability to see what's right in front of us. The restricted vision created by pain is a guaranteed recipe for more tragedies—creating more pain and increased hope-lessness if we fearfully move backwards in life. Our car, just like our life, was designed to advance on the road in front of it—into the future.

There is a special comfort and unique bonding that is created with others when we realize that someone faced the same painful situations we did. (The Holocaust, Vietnam War, physical abuse, rejection from family e.g.) We unknowingly seek out others that have faced the same events for comfort and greater understanding of ourselves and our life.

This can create a place of healing or a deeper pit of pity. When we desire pity we chose to live in the prison of past pain, literally turning a hurtful event into our life expectation. Healing lives above a painful event—pity lives in it.

Chapter Four

CHANGING OUR WORDS, SHIFTING OUR HEARTS

*Keep your heart with all diligence, for out of it
spring the issues of life (Pr. 4:23 NKJV).*

All of us have been surprised by the words we have said or
thought. Some words we stopped before they hit our tongue.
We have all confessed at one time or another, "I wish I would
have never said that."

> *For out of the abundance of the heart his mouth
> speaks (Luke 6:45 NKJV).*

We are to keep our hearts—with love and truth. Our hearts
cannot be restrained, but they can be retrained. Words flow out
from our hearts. Those words create our future. Controlling our
reactions and words is necessary at times, but it should not be
a way of life.

It's better to heal the damaged heart that creates those negative thoughts than restraining them from becoming our words on a frequent basis. That dynamic unchecked, starts building a religious spirit—right on the outside, wrong on the inside. Negative words that keep rising from our heart signal a need for a heart change.

When we are bumped in life what is in our hearts spills out. If our response is greater than the event, it points to the fact that we are carrying pain from the past that the Lord wants to heal. When the enemy uses people or situations to wound and discourage us, Father God is watching our response. If our response is based in His love, we are ready for greater assignments. If our reaction is based in selfishness, anger and hatred— we now have the opportunity to deal with what may have been hidden from our eyes.

Our reaction reveals what is blocking our intimacy with Him and the fullness of our purpose. What we do with that reaction determines if we become more religious or more anointed. Defending our reaction, leads to self-righteousness, hardness of heart and less authority. Allowing His Spirit to search our hearts expands our borders and increases His hand with us— like Jabez.

Decisions we make concerning our pain determines if we will be healed. It also defines our ability to bring healing to others. Otherwise we become the next one in line to pass our wounds onto others. Permanent victims of the past will become the abusers of others in the future even if it is in a different form or fashion.

Two healthy people became quadriplegics after horrific accidents. One person became a famous painter, the other one became a drug addict and a thief. Their response was pivotal in determining their future, not the tragedy they both encountered. The words from their hearts created their new season.

We must never forget the courage of faith and the force of vision that can take us past a tragedy into greatness. But make no mistake about it, it still would be a very difficult and painful situation for any of us to face. A great life never evolves from an easy life. All the wisdom I have gained was not from a cheap ticket.

The anointing and faith cannot operate fully when the words from our hearts condemn us. When we face pain in life it condemns us. It attempts to devalue our identity. In the banking industry, inflation occurs when the value of money decreases. What we could have possessed in the last season while shopping is now unavailable due to the lessening of value in the identity of each dollar. The value of our identity determines what we can possess in life, in His Kingdom.

> *For if our heart condemns us, God is greater than our heart, and knows all things. Beloved, if our heart does not condemn us, we have confidence toward God. 1 John 3:20, 21*

Our hearts do not condemn what we do, but who we are. This is the identity battle we cannot win without God's help. Condemning words from our hearts have power over us and our destiny. He is greater. He knows who we are and what He has planned for us. When our hearts agree with God on who we are, it comes is under His love and we have confidence towards God for our purpose.

Pain forces us forward—towards truth or to lies. We determine who will guide us through each painful experience. We can choose Jesus, the one who is love and truth—or the accuser of the brethren and deceiver of the world, Satan. Each one is trying to invade our thoughts. We might even believe that we can guide ourselves through it, which contains the element of pride, Satan's best stronghold.

We determine who will guide us by the attitudes we choose. We can even switch guides in the middle of the tour of our pain. It is not unusual and should be expected that both of these guides will interrupt the guide we have chosen at the beginning of the "tour of pain" to point out what they think is most important—trying to bring us to conclusions about life, ourselves and others.

One guide can own a greater portion of our life tour than another. Each one is trying to be the total owner on our "tour of pain;" Jesus, the healer and Satan, the accuser. Who and what we focus on the tour of pain determines how we think about ourselves and the future. We must be slow to assume that we see clearly through every part of the devastating and painful events. If we keep our eyes on Him, revelation will continue to unfold over time bringing us to greater freedom in each new season.

When we know the history of pain an abuser has carried for years, we can logically predict how they will treat people around them until they can think outside the pain and dark spirits that are now controlling them. If we carry pain, we will deliver pain. If we carry healing, we will deliver healing.

We will receive freedom from our abuse or become an abuser. There is no middle ground in our hearts or in the realm of the spirit—darkness or light. One will continue to increase to dominate the other. Our hearts must choose light to battle the pressing darkness that exists in our carnal flesh and this fallen world.

The identity on the inside of David gave him the authority to resist and overcome Goliath. David knew he was the future king of Israel, not the shepherd who died at the hands of Goliath. Our identity is foundational to the outcome of many battles. Our ability to dream past the pain of rejection and abandonment is the entrance to our destiny.

Pain Beyond Words

No one can fully know our pain, outside of Jesus. It is very difficult for any of us to put into words how we feel when we are literally in the midst of it. It is often surreal—beyond anything connected to previously known reality. Even if the circumstances are exactly the same, each of us will react differently based on previous wounds, fears and our unique strengths, and personality.

When my first wife passed away from cancer, people would ask me, "How are you doing?" First of all, I was thankful that I had many friends who cared enough to ask. I would share more details of my journey with my closer friends, but actually it was very difficult to understand all my emotions—let alone put them into words.

Great emotional pain triggers a partial shutdown to protect us from insanity. As the shutdown lifts, we must process the pain to remain healthy. We often respond to these inquires by saying, "I'm taking it one day at a time." What are we really saying? Long term vision must wait until we process the pain and loss we have just experienced.

Father God put a natural numbing effect into intense pain, physically and emotionally, to limit its ability to overpower and destroy us when it occurs. The pain of an event, physically or emotionally, can actually increase hours, days, weeks or years after the incident occurs. The numbing effect gives us the ability to function in the situation. As it lifts, we must deal with the pain to stay healthy and whole.

Father God brought LuAnne into my life as a gift to be my wife. I was startled by the amount of grief that I literally felt leave me the first time she kissed me. The continuous two year battle with cancer that preceded my first wife's death had built a grief that became my "normal." Fresh vision is filled with hope and joy. Love and new dreams will break off hidden grief. Bitterness and grief can also steal the dreams of our future.

"I am living the dream" is a phrase that is often spoken. Somehow we interpret it to mean that they have a pain free life. That is delusional at best, deceiving at its worst. The truth is they are living the dream in spite of the pain of the past and the present pain. "Living the dream" is never pain free, but it is wonderful.

If we believe that "living the dream" only belongs to those who have a pain free life, we will never fully engaged with the dream we are actually living—because we do not believe we have arrived. Pain deceives. If we arrive at our destination, but it does not look like the place we have pictured in our minds, we will keep on driving—looking for a place that does not exist. We will leave the place of fruitfulness where our dreams are to unfold, and enter into a wilderness, driven and deceived. Dreams are never pain free. Live the dream above the pain.

How can we describe pain? How do we measure the level of anyone's pain? It is impossible to chart in a comparative analysis. It is also difficult to know how much pain we still carry. Our reactions are nothing less than revealers of deep pain or deep healing. The amount of pain we are carrying may be hidden from our eyes so we can cope. We tend to avoid talking about it until we have a safe person with whom we can share it.

One of the reasons for hiding pain is not because we have trouble telling the truth—life simply feels unsafe. "Does anyone really care? If you knew what happened to me, would you still love me, treat me differently or blame me? If you knew what I did wrong, would you still love me?" Who can I trust? It is difficult to truly love ourselves, let alone trust others with our hearts.

We often struggle to love ourselves as well as understand ourselves. When others love us it makes it easier to love ourselves. That is one of the reasons why "He first loved us." Most people are waiting to be loved, but we are called to be like Jesus—to be the ones to love first. Be an ignitor of love.

The pain that tears at our hearts tells us that we are not valuable or loveable. If we were, they would not have hurt us. We forget that hurt people, hurt people. The enemy makes sure that rejection lands in a place in our heart that we are already struggling with internally.

We might have approached the abuser as a victim in the beginning that allowed the circumstances to escalate into a very hurtful situation, but that does not clear them or ourselves. We must own our part that was looking for acceptance in an unhealthy way or we will set ourselves up for more pain in the future.

We must also realize there are people that we might love who are not safe. Some of them are a part of our lives that we cannot totally avoid, but once we recognize the unhealthy patterns we are well on our way to a healthier relationship and living safer.

We do not need to sign up for someone's demands, thinking it will produce a better relationship. We must learn to give healthy gifts before the predictable demands to break the abuse/victim cycle. Somedays, just avoid them altogether.

Love cannot exist where the demands of others determines our value. That is nothing less than selling ourselves into emotional slavery. We are putting our value on the open market the enemy owns waiting for a response from others, instead of investing into others by the love of Christ that the enemy cannot touch or steal. What we give can never be stolen, only what we clutch fearfully can be taken.

Rejection pushes us to sell ourselves. The spirit of rejection can shout while trying to impress others or it can partially hide crying to manipulate the attention of others. The spirit of rejection will attempt to enlist the help of others through manipulating praise and controlling guilt.

Let's learn to rest in His love and give it to those around us. Jabez did not want to live in pain or from pain one more day. There is a day in each of our lives that we break stride with the fear that pain has created, like Jabez. Unselfish love produces close friends that Father God knew we would need in this life. Healthy friendships are significant to keeping dreams alive.

Jabez was noted as more honorable than his brothers. If his life was measured in light of his brothers you can be certain that they shared many of the same difficult situations with various differences. The collective pain had increased in the family to the tipping point that the mother named her one child, Jabez—pain.

Every time his mother would call his name that sounded like pain, a dishonoring spirit and negative thoughts of limitation to would invade Jabez's struggling identity. Pain produces a negative identity. Jabez could sense the impact it was having on his life. Pain will dissolve the honor from our identity until we break its grip until we cry out to the Lord in prayer, like Jabez.

Father God shattered the limitations carried in the devalued identity of Jabez that had been created by pain that was now warring against his anointed spirit, his faith in Father God, and the "heart of David" that desired to live his life through Him. Jabez did not want to live a normal life under pain, but the abundant life promised by the words of Jesus.

The choice Jabez made in prayer increased his identity to give him the ability to carry more honor with his life. The removal of pain from the life of Jabez was not the key to his new season—it was the shift in his identity as it came into the honor of the Lord that broke the power of the pain to control his thinking and dominate his spirit. Our spirit needs to be free to birth the dreams God placed in our hearts into our story for His glory.

The spirit of a man is the lamp of the Lord, searching all the inner depths of his heart.
Proverbs 20:27

Jabez was the only one in his family who made the identity shift at this time this was written that made him more honorable than his brothers who were still anchored with a negative identity that generated more pain. I would suspect this observation was written by an older man who did not live to see the full impact of Jabez's life to his brothers.

No two lives are ever the same, even in the same circumstances. If their father and mother had both died, they were raised by close relatives. It is probable that Jabez experienced more pain in his life than they did as his name reflects, yet he surpassed them in blessings. Many times a better life can keep us from a best life.

Pain is in the earth through man's selfishness and sin. Those components are resident in each of us as well, so from time to time we all cause pain at some level. The dark spirit of the enemy strategically whispers into our hurts attempting to destroy our destiny. Pain cannot be escaped in this life, but it can be overcome. Pain may not be as severe in our lives as it is in someone else's, but it is no less detrimental to how we see ourselves.

Time Frames of Life

The pain from a failure tries to mentally block our faith from trying or even dreaming again. It attempts to short-circuit what God has called us to do in our life. Pain is one of the tools of the enemy uses to limit our identity and assignments.

Jesus bore our pain on the cross and the effects it produced—hopelessness, shame and fear. These elements are dream breakers and identity deformers.

Pain breaks our ability to trust. When painful events occur there is often a strong a sense of betrayal. If we cannot trust others, it is very difficult to be a part of effective teamwork that is required to accomplish great things.

Pain can only span from the past and into the present. We can be in pain right now. We cannot be in pain from what has happened in the future, even though we can experience pain from the fear of the future. Faith is now and goes into the future. Faith is not active in the past, because it cannot change the past.

Revelation can help us see our past differently as it changes our assumptions, but not the event. When we see our past in the light of revelation, it changes our conclusions about our life and ourselves. It actually changes our view of Father God in our past, which shifts our view of Him in our future. That upgrades our view of life with Father God that dynamically intensifies our relationship with Him which opens up endless possibilities. Pain lies about Him to steal our destiny.

What does this tell us? Faith will not change our past any more than pain can change our future unless we choose to carry it into the future. Faith and pain are in the *now*. We must choose what we will carry forward into our future.

If we chose to continue to carry pain, then our future will look like our past. If we chose to carry hope each day, we will experience a series of events that will form a new season in His love, grace and favor. Carrying pain is hard work, with no rewards. Let's not be pain carriers, but glory carriers—because His glory will carry us in difficult times.

Faith visions the future, but pain stares at the past. Both are active in this present moment, in this window of time. The way we embrace each of them will determine our destiny. His love desires to bring healing to our past. The more healed we are, the easier it is to step into our new assignments. Limitations are shattered through healing the past and renewing our faith. Dream again!

> *Now faith is the substance of things hoped for, the evidence of things not seen. For by it the elders obtained a good testimony. By faith we understand that the worlds were framed by the word of God, so that the things which are seen were not made of things which are visible (Hebrews 11:1-3 NKJV).*

Now faith is—denotes an access point in time that faith is available to all of us, *now*. Pain cannot create your future, only negative faith has that ability. Pain attempts to create a negative faith by reviewing our disappointing past and announcing our future as the same. No one can choose to carry pain and live in faith. Unresolved pain is very damaging to our "now faith."

The enemy uses pain as one of the greatest vision limiters. Pain creates unbelief as lies seem more real than truth. Our faith has the ability to walk us past pain into the future before our hurts are totally resolved. Father God is giving us a heaven experience to detract from the hell experience because we believed Him beyond the pain. Let that victory break the grip of the enemy's lies. In our quest to gain more faith, let's dump the pain. Our creativity and faith will soar with vision when pain is removed from our spirit and mind.

Father God will utilize the pain the enemy brings against us to awaken our hearts. Will we choose to step into the favor and goodness He has available? Pain is a part of death as well as birthing. Our choices determine which it will be. Death in our present season can also be the birthing of our new season as we look to Him and not the pain. Our identity speaks our future. We must not let pain change our identity or our dreams in these intense emotional battles.

Let's declare these words with our hearts: *I am choosing to not carry the pain of my past into my future. I am choosing to not allow the pain of the past to carry me away from my destiny or limit me. Father God, I focus on you and not the pain, the enemy brought to destroy me.*

You are turning the enemies' attempt to bring death in my present season into a birthing season with new mercies and favor. You are my Father, the God of surprise victories. I give all my pain to Jesus who loves me and bore it in His body, for me, on the cross. Jesus, reveal to me anywhere I am still carrying pain or it is carrying me so that I can live totally in You and the fullness of my destiny.

I am using "now faith" to break through the cycle of pain by trusting You, dwelling in You and entering into that which You have prepared for me. Pain, you will not change the way I see myself or my future. Pain, you will not steal my dreams. Father God, you are my inheritance and the one who declared my identity and my purpose. Everything required for my destiny lies in You. I receive You—I give You—me. Let my faith soar in the dreams You have for me.

Chapter Five

PAIN, THE TEACHER AND THE LIMITER

After counseling and observing a man in my church for several years who struggled with depression and negative self-worth, the root issue to his struggles came out of his mouth; "Nothing I do ever works." I reflected on the his college degree that qualified him for a lucrative job that he enjoyed for years before he lost it, and now he could not even hold menial jobs. He would get job after job, where he was under-employed, only to lose them.

The Lord revealed to me a startling truth. I looked him straight in the eyes and said, "In all my years of pastoring, I have never seen anyone with as great of faith as you." His face slightly contorted with doubt. I continued. "Everything you believe is coming to pass. You have faith that you will get a job far beneath your expertise; you'll hate and then lose it. It happens every time just like you believe."

I knew that the truth I spoke to him shifted something inside him. He shortly thereafter moved to take a good job offer. Several years later he was employed in the profession of his college degree, a great job. He had great faith, but it was negative. We will not get what we want—we will get what we believe, even if it's wrong.

Pain produces limitations. Discipline that is reinforced with some pain can be a healthy teacher and a limiter of negative patterns as a child and even sometimes as an adult. It teaches us not to engage in those words or activities again. Parents should use different types of corrections that included some form of pain to train their younger children. It can range from a spanking to a time out followed by a loving celebration of that child's identity and life principles instructions to their heart.

The enemy can also use pain to derail us from destiny. Pain can lie to us and about us. Pain is very believable, but not very reasonable. Pain can steal our brilliance or diminish it.

Pain can be a thief. It can also be a teacher. We must understand the positive aspects before we explore the downside. Lack of clarity in these two aspects of pain can produce costly errors in our thinking.

As we grow up, we learn not to touch hot things after a painful experience. We are more careful on a ladder after falling off of it. After being through a storm on a boat, we prioritize checking the weather before boating the next time and observing the weather while on the boat. Painful experiences can give us wisdom for the future.

Here is the problem: If a dream ends up in a painful situation, we become afraid to dream. We live too safe. We are not willing to trust Father God for an adventurous journey with high goals sprinkled with huge problems that required several miracles. A life of purpose will challenge us to great faith while building character in us.

Why do the scriptures reveal that God faith is rooted in love? If our faith is rooted in pain, its fruit is defiled. The love of God conquers the pain of the past as we chose to forgive others, ourselves and release our future to His love.

His love for us shatters our judgments against Him and against ourselves. One of the enemies' most effective schemes is to create judgments against ourselves and God through painful experiences. These two judgments are lethal dream killers and destiny limiters.

We may feel we have a pretty normal life, but we were called to the extraordinary. Good is not good enough. Good is less than God's best. Good is boring. A good life is the arch enemy to an amazing life. When our life moves from bad to good be thankful, but keep moving towards amazing.

If we live a safe life it will become so boring that sin seems more exciting and we are more easily tempted. When David was resting from war, he fell. When David was facing Goliath, being pursued by King Saul, or taking Jerusalem from the Jebusites to be the City of David he was very focused with faith as he was moving towards his destiny. Bored people do crazy and are critical.

When we are tempted by the enemy we should not just say no to the temptation. We should move past it, delete it, not say it, or even think it—then look towards heaven and say, "This is my worship and my love for You. I am saying *"yes"* to increase of my anointing. I am saying *"yes"* to my destiny. I am saying *"yes"* to our intimate relationship." A *"yes"* life is more powerful than a *"no"* life. A *"no"* will keep us from doing wrong, but a "yes" will keep us doing right. It can be dangerous to be parked in front of temptation with only a "no."

An advancing life requires a passionate pursuit that creates holiness. It takes an intimate relationship with Father God to accomplish our God dreams and assignments. That alone pushes out the strange loves that exist in this world that are trying to connect with our carnal flesh. Forgiveness keeps us from choking the anointing we have, breaking tormenting spirits from our lives.

There is greater angelic activity protecting me when I am in the middle of His will. David was safer running towards Goliath than walking on his roof top where he saw Bathsheba. Living safer in the natural is overrated. A dangerous destiny in God is well protected with high rewards.

We must make a choice, like Jabez, to stop living in and from the pain of the past. When the love of God replaces the pain of the past, faith in God can take deep roots in our lives giving us the ability to adventure in life with the expectation of victory. Pain short-circuits our ability to handle more responsibilities. The healthy advance His kingdom. His kingdom is within us and His glory is through us.

Now is the time for us to breakthrough any limitations that sorrow and pain have produced. The pain could be a result of our own poor decisions, circumstances beyond our control and/ or hurtful situations created by people around us. Normally all of these are intertwined because we make the worst decisions when we face our deepest fears and wounds. If we listen to the Holy Spirit we will break our natural life patterns of self-defense that continue to recycle us into painful situations again. Remember, pain tells us something is wrong. Change is needed.

Pain starts from an event in our childhood that we naturally bury to emotionally survive. The pain and the shame are
repeated in a variety of situations with the same theme. Our
life is overshadowed with hopelessness in a specific area from
that repeated theme. We can settle for less without a battle.
We can believe the lie that it's useless—or we can choose to
breakthrough.

Pain cannot be our life instructor. Pain is embedded with
fear. Fear is a dictator. It demands that we live in a place of
great shelter, a cave, trying to avoid past hurts. Fear lies to us.
The "cave of fear" promises to make our life safer while it naturally prepares another traumatic event. One of the main problems with caves: no natural windows for vision. Number two:
it's all about survival from the enemy. A life of destiny takes
down the enemy.

Fear cannot bring us to safety. Fear opens the door to more
pain and disappointments. Only His love and His wisdom
provide safety in a world of pain. His love crushes our fears
bringing a release to our spirit and mind to dream again. The
victories of heaven break the darkness of hell that wars to steal
our God dreams. Carry the dream, until the dream carries you.

*Prayer: Father God, I am coming out of my cave of pain
by the power of Your Spirit. In the name of Jesus, pain, you
cannot steal my dreams and my purpose. I break every negative
thought that is stealing my future. Because I have the Spirit of
God, I have the thoughts of God. I receive Your genius into my
life. I refuse to live a hidden life for false safety. I hide my life
in my Father God, who is my safety. I open my spirit to dream*

in Your Spirit beyond the pain. I receive the destiny I have to live in You, Father God.

Crying Out to Our Father

We must cry out to Father God to halt the pain that has ruled over our lives. It will not stop until we face the Goliath of our pain with a deep desire for change. David engaged Goliath verbally before taking him on the battle. Our words must define who we are to Father God before we engage the *"intimidator."* David ran towards Goliath who put fear on the entire army of Israel. God is maturing and anointing *"Davids"* to shatter the fear that has come over His people.

There comes multiple times in our lives where we must cry out to Father God or lose the opportunity that is possible at that moment. It's beyond the prayer we use to obtain the things we need. It is intercession for our core identity and the importance of our life purpose.

It is a cry of our spirit with words that comes from the core of our being—filled with truth and covered with His anointing. It is deep and it is loud. That cry of intercession is for our destiny and the purposes of heaven that God placed within us.

There is prayer in that cry, plus much more—everything you are, is reaching up to everything He is. Our value is regained in His presence. Wisdom and direction that affects our entire life unfolds inside of us. Relationships are restored. Relationships that have never existed are created to open doors to God dreams.

There are plans and preparation required to reach every dream, but some will only be entered through divine interruptions. Those startling events first appear as an over-whelming tragedy or deep loss. It will bring us to our knees and to the end of ourselves—and a beginning in Him. Unexpected events will take us deeper into Him if we will make Him our total source. That response brings heaven into our hell.

There may have been heart breaking events that brought more pain into Jabez's life driving him into a secret place with God where he had never been before, shifting the depth and focus of his prayer changing everything touching his life forever.

First responders take care of those suffering the greatest pain first, expecting the other first responders or medical personal that are unexpectedly present to help. No one expects someone in great pain at a tragic accident to help others in danger, but many times that occurs. They are the heroes of disasters because they lived above the pain they were experiencing to help others. There are times we will have to live in that paradigm—be one of His heroes.

Those that place their lives in danger to bring others to safety are always esteemed. This is the mark of a "more honorable life." When we place the life critical needs of others before our excruciating pain, honor is given to us by the coldest of hearts.

Jesus chose to bear our pain in the Garden of Gethsemane. I know He did more, but I want us to stop and focus on this one issue. He desired to take away our pain. According to Isaiah 53:4, Jesus bore our pain so we would not have to carry it our entire lives.

We are not helplessly stuck in a quagmire of pain in this life because of the great love of Jesus and the personal sacrifice He chose. We must also chose to live in Him—His value of us, His thoughts about us and His plans for us. He is our safe place in an unsafe world.

There is a love beyond pain—even in the midst of it. His love and forgiveness works in the most painful situations. These elements produce a wisdom that is beyond us and this world that produces miracles. What God is about to do is beyond us, but not without us. Dream again. Dream more often.

Forgiveness can be hard, but life is overwhelming without it. Living a life of unforgiveness is the most hellish life possible on this earth. The enemy on the inside is more detrimental and debilitating than the enemy on the outside.

The scriptures tell us there will be no pain in heaven. Heaven is only heaven because God the Father, Jesus Christ and Holy Spirit have created an atmosphere that Satan cannot shift. It's not about a place, it's about them. Live in Christ and experience heaven on earth. That does not mean that you have a pain free life, but rather free from the control and limitations it produces.

If we continue to tolerate our circumstances in our spirit, we will never shift our lives with an intimate prayer that moves heaven into our lives. A desperate believing heart that prays in faith will open the heavens for God's favor and blessings to pour on our lives—just like Jabez.

When we cry out to Father God with the heart of Jabez, the faith of Jabez and the principles in his prayer, Father God will shift us into a new season of blessing and increase—just like He did for Jabez. Sometimes we are waiting for God to bring the gas station to our house and fill up our car that is parked in the garage.

The truth is that most all cars are filled in the process of a journey. Start your engine, start your journey—even with a half tank of gas. The gas we need for our complete journey is only available to us as we journey.

There is a cry from the heart that catches the attention of all heaven. It must come from the depths of our spirit, from the center of our passion. There is a sense of worship in the intensity of that request that actually honors Father God as the source of our life. We must be taught how to cry out to God after being told all of our lives not to cry—even girls have been told this, but especially boys.

Hezekiah cried out to God when he was told by Isaiah the prophet to put his house in order as he was about to die. Hezekiah cried out to God. As Isaiah was leaving, God turned him around in the middle of courtyard of the king's palace as he was leaving to tell Hezekiah that God gave him fifteen more years of life. Hezekiah's heart cry shifted the word of the Lord concerning his life span in the same hour.

Father God turned time backwards to let the king know that his cry was heard. Hezekiah and Jabez had something in common: the cries of their hearts that released breakthrough.

Jabez prayed—but his prayer became the cry of his heart. Jabez was not mourning. His deep intense desire for change was gaining volume in his heart. The cry of his heart was the force behind this astounding prayer. The shout that brought down the walls of Jericho was in the midst of the cry of his heart.

There was a bold faith that reached into the heavens as he cried out to Father God with a loud voice. It's time to gain full access to our destiny. Let's stop crying to ourselves and others.

We still have our voice—let's use it to cry out to Father God like Jabez—loudly, with passion.

Prayer: Holy Spirit, create the cry and passion of Jabez in my heart that shatters the limitations built by the pain of my past. Father God, I want everything you have for me. Break me free from my past pain and bless me. I realized that my life is lacking. I am not satisfied to continue living under the pain I have experienced, nor the limitations it has produced over my life. I know you will give me more as I come before You this day and cry out to You. I will not remain silent until I receive Your best for me. Good is not good enough for me. You have more for me and I want it. Bless me beyond all measures that I have ever known.

Get alone in a private place and cry out with this prayer. It can be prayed more than once. It is a prayer that must gain momentum and volume in our hearts.

The Prison of Pain

Pain will steal our destiny and greatness. Prisons are filled with people who carried pain and caused pain. Life is filled with people who carry pain and caused pain—it becomes their prison—a prison of pain. No one can fulfill their destiny imprisoned in pain. It is time to have a jailbreak. Of all those imprisoned in the earth, only a small portion is behind steel bars.

As I was sharing a story with a pastor that I had just talked about several days before, I heard the Lord speaking to me: "Why are you talking about this again?" I had not mentioned this story to anyone for months, possibly years. I suddenly realized that there was still pain around this story at a much deeper level than I realized. I had previously forgiven the person, but I never saw it before that moment.

We cannot deal with issues until the Lord brings them to our attention or we realize that something is not right. He knows the perfect time for us to go deeper on the same issue. Out of the abundance of our hearts we speak. So when we start talking about a situation or a person with negative emotions, it signals that we need an oil change—now.

I was actively pursuing a new season of dreams with now faith and Father God was revealing to me a pain that I had not faced. I knew if I ignored the pain that was present it would limit my thinking and faith—intercepting or hindering my transition. My response to the problem was a greater block than what they had done. Father God wanted this pain and the lie it had created to sabotage my dreams to be decimated so my destiny advancement would be unhindered. Jabez dumped the pain before the Lord—then he entered a new season of blessings.

I shared the pain and repented of my judgments towards another prophet that I had carried from an event the pastor and the prophet both attended. They had become great friends. As I revisited my story, I sensed a deeper peace and a greater anointing come over my life. If we are telling our hurtful story to someone, we have also qualified them to be part of our healing. We must move from the need for validation of our identity and have a mature repentance that has the ability to focus on our judgments and responses, and not be distracted by what they did that was questionable.

It was not a major infraction or a big deal, but it was a deeper hurt than I wanted to admit, that had quietly built up over years. It was wonderful to be rid of that hidden offensive weight that was a destiny blocker for my new season.

There are many inner healing ministries that will reveal the Lord as the "Great Counselor." God uses them to bring us to greater healing and freedom, just as a Bible school brings us into a greater anointing. Healing and anointing do not all happen at once—yet they do. Each requires the same process to bring forth the fullness of what He has done in our lives—and is still doing. Greater glory encounters will also drive pain out or to the surface. There is deliverance and counseling required to reach our destiny. It is the truth that sets us free.

God does not require a twelve step program to be free or even Bible College to learn more about Him, but they are equally helpful and there are many variations for each individual. We must keep in step as we journey with Father God as He brings issues to our attention to keep momentum in His Spirit. Our hearts cannot shift without His dealings and our personal pursuit of Him. Every Christian has been counseled and trained in a variety of ways.

As judgmental pain is removed, we have a greater capacity to carry His glory. He must increase and I must decrease—that is a process request in the life of one of the greatest prophets that ever lived, John the Baptist. Decreasing is not an event, but a process containing events. Father God is the Great Counselor as well as the Mighty God—know Him as both. We will either carry the weight of His glory or the weight of our pain.

Jabez – More Honorable

> *Now Jabez was more honorable than his brothers, and his mother called his name Jabez, saying, "Because I bore him in pain." And Jabez called on the God of Israel saying, "Oh, that You would bless me indeed, and enlarge my territory, that Your hand would be with me, and that You would keep me from evil, that I may not cause pain!" So God granted him what he requested. 1 Chron. 4:9, 10 NKJV*

Jabez sounds like the Hebrew word for *pain*. It is impossible to live a life of honor with our minds focused on pain. The more pain we carry it proportionally diminishes the honor we are able to receive or give. Honorable lives are not pain free. However, we cannot allow painful situations to change how we see ourselves or others.

We cannot permit pain to steal our peace and joy in undesirable circumstances. If it does, it signals that our identity is determined by our circumstances, not God's presence. Our identity is deformed in oppressive circumstances without His life in our identity. We will not have the ability to manage our promised land until we can handle the giants on them. The scripture below reveals that the ten spies saw the land devouring them as well as the giants.

> *And they gave the children of Israel a bad report of the land which they had spied out, saying, "… it is a land that devours its inhabitants…; and*

106

*we were like grasshoppers in our own sight, and
so we were in their sight." Numbers 13:32, 33*

How we see ourselves is how others see us as well. If we
feel certain that people treat us in a negative fashion, make
sure they are not connecting to a negative identity issue that is
residing within us. The majority of the time, most people will
honor us according to the honor we have received from God.

Insecurity, with an underlying sense of rejection, is death
to our destiny—and the enemy knows it, so he creates events
that feed these issues. Our focus on Father God establishes
our value and acceptance that crushes the enemies lies based
in past disappointments and humiliations. Father God's love
births acceptance, honor and value that release His abundance
into our destiny.

Carrying pain produces a broken spirit and a negative
attitude that will control us. It will attempt to defend us by
destroying others when we feel threatened, which only brings
greater loss to our purpose. As every good farmer knows, we
can only sow this season what was reaped in the last season.
If we bless others who hurt us, we have seeds of blessings that
produce much fruit.

All of us must overcome negative family patterns and
curses that the enemy created to keep the generations of our
family line from reaching their destiny. We are breaking out of
generational limiting cycles of frustration, like Jabez did from
his family. We also must recognize the blessings that are in
our family generations that we must embrace through revelation so we can expand them. A judgement against our family,
especially our parents, releases a curse over our lives that can

intercept our blessings or minimalize them. Forgiveness is required for blessings to overtake us.

Carrying emotional pain from the past in a specific area blurs or blocks our ability to see into the future in that same specific area. Any area of life in which we carry pain, it is hard to expand and advance. If we hide our pain behind another area where we are successful, that blessing becomes an idol as the source of our well-being. God will remove it sooner or later so that we make Him the full source of our life. He desires increasing depth in His intimate relationship with us—amazing.

Only Jesus could carry the honor of Father God above the pain of the cross. He saved a thief and forgave those who crucified Him in the midst of the pain. He did not attack those who were attacking him. He loved and died above the pain of the cross—while the nails still pierced Him.

He died in honor to the Father and in love with the world. This is why Jesus is unstoppable. Jesus defeated pain and the shame, created by sin, at the cross. The blood He shed on the cross therefore sets us free from the guilt, the pain and the shame of sin. We ask His forgiveness and receive His righteousness, our innocence is restored. We receive His healing for the pain, and we walk in His delight. We break the spirit of shame and receive a double honor from Him.

We often receive forgiveness for our sins, but we often carry the shame of that sin—an unbearable emotional weight. Shame steals our identity and purpose. It crushes our heart, stealing our faith for the future. Receive the fullness of what Jesus accomplished on the cross. As a song says, "My sin is gone, I've been set free!" He expects us to live privileged. It's a compliment to His goodness and ability

Can you imagine living a shame free and pain free life? From the suffering of the cross, He crushed death and sat on the throne at the right hand of Father God. He paid the price for our total freedom. We are about to shattered the limitations of pain!

Declare this: He has taken my sin and I receive His righteousness, my innocence is restored. I receive His healing for the pain, and I walk in the comfort and delight of the Holy Spirit. I break the spirit of shame in the name of Jesus and live in a double honor. His love rests on me. I am favored. His greatness is in me and empowering the destiny that He created for me. He celebrates me. He blesses me. His love gives value and honor to my life empowering me to live a bold destiny. I live privileged. My destiny empowers others reach their destiny.

Chapter Six

THE FIVE POINTS OF JABEZ'S HEART CRY

Oh, That You Would Bless Me

Jabez asked Father God to bless his *"me."* If our worship of Father God does not include thankfulness for the *"me"* He has made us, it is a form of judgment against Him and ourselves. Celebrating Father God and who He created us to be is honoring to Him and it empowers us to reach our destiny. If we do not celebrate who He has made us, we cannot truly celebrate others as a tint of jealousy and envy are still lodged in our hearts.

Jabez was not asking Father God for a particular blessing concerning a present need, but rather a blessing for his *"me,"* shifting his identity. There is a stark different in these two types of requests. The first request is problem based, the second one is vision based.

Jabez had lived under negative words and negative situations that probably felt as if he was fighting the *curse of less.*

His mother had named him out of pain connecting a curse to his identity. Jabez wanted a blessing to break the curse that seemed to rest on his family and particularly on his "me." There is a blessing that will overcome every curse and hurt the enemy has brought onto our life.

Jabez chose the blessing to reverse the curse that existed in his identity. Jabez was not being self-centered when he requested that Father God to bless him. He had a revelation that God's blessing would break the curse. This would be one of the strategic keys to produce a quantum leap in his identity.

Emotional pain will derail or distort our natural identity development that is necessary to reach our full destiny. Until we absolutely receive the blessing of the Lord deep into our physical being, reasoning and spirit, the inner tension of the pain will limit our ability to step into our greater seasons. We should never stop with success, but leverage it to the greatness of our destiny that He has called us to live.

If we are healed from our wounds, but our wounded identity is not shifted to a blessed identity, our wounded identity will simply produce and align for more wounding experiences. It is not a lack of intelligence or information, but rather it is the lack of a healthy identity. We need our "me" to be blessed to live blessed. **Prayer:** *Father bless my identity, bless my "me", as I go from glory to glory so I can bring You honor in every season with my life.*

Our identity sets up our assignments. We are not call to live out of what we have, but rather who we are. The celebration of the Lord in our lives causes us to see who we are to Him— and others. Where others celebrate us is the place we should stand to experience our next elevation and new assignments. A healthy identity fuels our journey into destiny.

Jabez wanted the Lord to bless him. This was a request for an intimate relationship with God and to experience the richness and liberty that dwells in Him. Abundance without a relationship with Him is nothing but more stuff. Our successes can mock our lost identity. Our possessions will taunt our emptiness if we are disconnected from the reality of His love and true life.

Abundance is a love relationship that overflows in every aspect concerning our lives and our needs—and yes even our desires. I will get things for my wife beyond her needs that are her desires, because of my love for her. Father God is better than me—way better. Expect His love to bring you more. The small details in His blessings reveal His amazing love for us.

What we obtain by our own ability will never be as precious as what others give to us with love. Without love, whatever we have is not a treasure—it is only riches.

Abundance is more than you need, not more than what someone else has. The Father gives us more than what we need to bless others. The greatest gifts are always surpassed by smaller gifts with love. Until we live beyond ourselves towards others, life is fairly boring. We need to ask God to bless us so we can bless others. When we make Him our source, then we have resources available to us that are out of this world.

Many of us will work for blessings, but we will not ask Him for the same. Pride and self-reliance are at the core of our efforts. He has blessed us with talents and abilities that we are to use, but without His love as our life those abilities drive us as slaves in the world of success—trying to prove our value.

We become orphans instead of experiencing His delight that belongs to *"sons and daughters."* I cover many of these truths in my book, "Two Sons and a Father."

Changing jobs or quitting all together is not the solution, but rather requesting His more. More of Him comes with more of everything. He helps us reach our destiny as we are building our purpose in Him.

Some of us may be uncomfortable with asking Father God to bless us, but actually He desires that we would make our requests known to Him. We pride ourselves on being self-sufficient, but it is also demonic in nature. Humility asks for His help. It builds a working relationship that is filled with revelation.

We were designed to be interdependent within Father God. Let's run after God until we are running in Him and He is running through us. David did not just see God as a warrior as he ran towards Goliath, he saw God as a warrior in him. When David ran towards Goliath, so did Father God.

Enlarge My Territory

Jabez did not want to live small. When we think small and live small we "small" God down to this world. Jabez desired to live beyond the limitations of his present life. Are we content to settle for less for our entire lives? Complacency should not be confused with contentment.

We need to enlarge our territory in adverse times. If we have a need for medical attention, we should also be aware of the needs of others we pass in the hospital. A self-centered life is a dark hole that sucks the joy out of life. I challenge you to look for an opportunity to encourage someone. A giving life is an exciting life.

When the Father expands our territory, it connects us to more people with new assignments. Esther was elevated by Father God when she was chosen to be queen by the king. It removed the orphan status and limitations it placed over her life. She was blessed to be the queen, but its purpose had not yet been revealed to her. Like Esther, an unexpected promotion is often for an unknown assignment.

Father God expanded her identity and her territory to touch a moment in history that would preserve a people and a nation. He restored her identity by the king and gave her the ability to influence history. We must be aware that when Father God connects us to people of greater honor it expands our territory for a greater life purpose. Ultimately it presents us with a greater responsibility for a greater number of people involving more difficult situations requiring greater wisdom.

Removing negative thoughts and limitations that we or others have placed over our lives enlarges our territory. We must have an identity shift to enter and possess our increased territory. I cover this concept in my first book, "And David Perceived He Was King."

We need to ask Father God to enlarge our territory to impact and influence the world around us. A core value of the gospel is to go into the world. We must build up the church while reaching the world. Who we are in Christ is foundational, but who we are in this world is purposeful to advancing His kingdom.

As we advance in our destiny we open our past positon to someone who is also advancing. Hopefully we can train others to do what we have done as we enlarge our territory. Pioneers open up territories that others may continue to build up and eventually settle or become the pioneers for the next generation. Do we really want Father God to enlarge our territory? We are asking for greater responsibility, an increased workload, numerous complex problems, significant finances will be required, more advanced planning with greater vision, a larger team to complete the budding task in unity, increased delegation, more innovative ways to assist others and a deeper joy if we do it with excellence. Do we still want it? Yes, I want it. Enlarge my territory, Lord.

Let Your Hand Be With Me

The third thing that Jabez asks for was that God's hand would be with him. Jabez knew that he needed help from Father God to expand his territory. He looked to God for His ability, protection, presence and guidance in his life.

We need the hand of God with us to open doors to our future by connecting us to the right people at the right time concerning the right purpose. His hand brings us into situations as well as getting us out of others. Let Your hand be with us, Father God.

When His hand is with us it increases the authority in our words, the wisdom in our decisions, the direction in our journey of life, creating momentum in the vision, miracles that sustain our purpose and peace in the midst of unsolved problems.

"We do not seek your hand, we only seek your face" is a line from a famous worship song. That vital truth comes from the scriptures, but we must understand that Jabez's request was from a different desire.

First we must understand that seeking His hand is not the same as requesting His hand to be with us. Seeking His hand is focusing on what He can give us versus seeking Him. Jabez was requesting that the hand of God would be with him, not what the hand of God could bring him. Jabez desired Father God's hand of strength through and in his life.

It is another way of asking God's presence to be with him just as Moses did. Jabez was asking God's hand, *God's ability and His strength*, to always be present in his life. Moses had experienced God's presence and saw His mighty power in the midst of his call at the burning bush, but he interceded that God's presence would continue to go with them after Israel worshiped the golden calf. The mercy of God is awesome.

Jabez did not want an average life or just a good life. He desired a God life. He desired the presence and the power of God with him—the hand of God. Jabez desired Father God's hand to be evident in his deeds and actions. Just do it through my life. He did not ask for Father God to increase his strength, but desired His strength.

Jabez was a man of action and he wanted to see the exploits of heaven around his life. He was not going to sit back and live a life of pain just because of the trauma in his life. He was shedding the negative identity from the name his mother had chosen for him. He had a greater vision than to just simply be free of pain. Jabez wanted the purposes of God in his life with power.

The power of Father God breaks the power of pain. Often we experience pain when we are the weaker or less significant person among others. Pain comes into our life when we relied on our strength or the strength of someone else, not His. Our strength can be a weakness and absolutely destructive if we are not submitted to the Holy Spirit. Sin destroyed the Garden of Eden, but His presence can restore a life of wonders.

It takes the power of Father God to move us beyond the pain of the past. His power is based in His love for us. His love heals our wounded heart and identity so that we can bring healing love to others.

The hand of God was over Israel as He delivered them from Egypt, but they had not yet entered His presence. Therefore God's people could not stand against the giant to possess their Promised Land. Our response to the giants standing in the middle of our destiny will determine if we will be wilderness wanders or a Joshua generation.

The news of the giants brought back the pain of the bondage they had experienced in Egypt. The memory of that pain brought a tremendous fear into God's people. Fear will keep us in the wilderness. The wilderness is a place of miracles that will sustain us. It is free from giants and devoid of destiny.

We are not looking at our destiny until we see a giant standing in front of us. Run like David towards the giant. It takes a giant to reveal a David. Giants actually cause us to speak like Caleb, "Give me my mountain." His mountain was covered with several giants—probably one of the best properties of the Promised Land as giants get whatever they want. Destiny is never easy, but it is always worth it.

Can we see His hand above the giants or do we just see our heads beneath the giants? Father God, may your hand be with me. Where He leads us, He plans victory. It may be the same day or it could be another season, but He never allows defeat to be permanent. Our past failures do not have the ability to block our future success unless we let it degrade our identity and steal our dreams.

Jabez was tired of the hands of people and the strength of his hands. He wanted to see the hand of God move in his life. Father God honored his request. It is our Father's desire to do this for all His sons and daughters.

> *For the eyes of the LORD run to and fro throughout the whole earth, to show Himself strong on behalf of those whose heart is loyal to Him. 2 Chronicles 16:9*

He is searching throughout all the earth to find someone through whom He can show himself strong—one who is loyal to Him. Greatness will never be held over time by those who are not loyal to God and others. Let's be one of those He is searching for to show Himself strong.

> *And the hand of the Lord was with them, and a great number believed and turned to the Lord. Acts 11:21 NKJV*

When the hand of the Lord is with us, it has a great impact on many people causing them to believe. Our identity and our unique assignments were designed to turn people's attention to the Lord.

> *The hand of the Lord came upon me and brought me out in the Spirit of the Lord, and set me*

*down in the midst of the valley; and it was full
of bones. Ezekiel 37:1 NKJV*

The hand of the Lord will take us to places of loss and death to speak life to dead dry bones. His hand does not always take us to wonderful places, but rather places that need His wonders. The hand of God will set us in challenging situations to make a difference. We do not ask for His hand to be with us for an easy life, but for a fulfilling life. His hand is with us for a fruitful life—that includes plowing, planting, weeding, irrigating and harvesting. Father, use our lives to bring Your life. *Oh that Your hand would be with us!*

Keep Me From Evil

Jabez requested that Father God keep him from evil. He was not just asking for a blessing over his life for personal gain, but he desired a more intimate walk with Father God. Here we can compare the prayer of Jabez with the Lord's Prayer "lead us not into temptation, but deliver us from the evil one" (Matthew 6:13).

Pain seeks temporary pleasure for relief. Additive lifestyles are often created to attain happiness. They cannot be conquered without healing the pain that has seated itself in our identity. Our love for people trapped in these self-destructive vices gives us the opportunity to apply truth that sets them free. Love without truth is ineffective and truth without love is defective.

Sin is a time robber and dream drainer. We fall behind schedule when we waste our time and energy with negative attitudes and actions, instead of capturing the moments that create momentum. We often then force ourselves to try to catch up instead of repenting and requesting that Father God restore to us the time, focus and momentum stolen by the enemy.

Our love for Father God should be the basis for personal holiness. Otherwise we can enter into a spirit of legalism and self-righteousness. Our active worship keeps us in step with heaven's calendar of destiny for our life. Expect more anointed appointments, divine interruptions and destiny advancing connections.

Jabez understood that his prayer for increase also carried other kinds of risks. The risk of falling into the evils of pride, self-sufficiency and the love of power that attempts to intercept and destroy us in the midst of our blessings. Pride started in the one created to lead the worship in heaven, a pretty nice place. Instead of leading worship, Lucifer led a rebellion.

Jabez asks that he would not be a pain—after receiving his blessings. Our continual worship blocks the strategic attacks of the one who refused to worship, strategic attacks to destroy our identity and destiny. Our worship releases heaven's best to flow to us and through us. Our purpose is advancing in the winds of heaven.

So That I Will Not Cause Pain

The central theme of the prayer of Jabez was to live a life free of pain. The last thing he ever wanted to do was to cause pain to others. He had suffered under it so long and he knew the devastation it produced. A holy life is a whole life that releases the goodness of God to those around us. It becomes a healing balm we offer to those we meet. That is one of the major reasons he prayed, "Keep me from evil."

Jabez was born in pain (1 Chronicles 4:9) and his name means "sorrow-maker". Jabez asked for God's blessing and expansion to his destiny. This shows us that his motivations came from a genuine heart filled with concern for others and not just his own well-being. Father God challenges us to have a vision to live beyond ourselves.

Jabez walked in love towards others by loving Father God first. That allowed Father God's love to flow to him and from him towards others. Father God's love protects us from the debilitating effects of pain and its invasion into our identity. The Father God's love in us releases many blessings to others supernaturally. It empowers our identity and anoints our activity. It embraces our life with hope that overflows on others. The blessings of Jabez are designed to impact earth with the blessings of Father God.

And God Granted His Request

God honored Jabez's request. God desires to give us the longings of our hearts because He is *"Our Father."* As sons and daughters who are maturing in His heart, we start to consider the longings of His heart. Each of us was designed to display His heart in a unique way.

> *Keep on asking, and you will receive what you ask for. Keep on seeking, and you will find. Keep on knocking, and the door will be opened to you. For everyone who asks, receives. Everyone who*

seeks, finds. And to everyone who knocks, the door will be opened. Matthew 7:7-8, (NLT)

Jabez prayed for his success. Some might feel uncomfortable with this concept as a biblical principal. If we do not pray for our success, how can we effectively pray success for others? It would be the same as praying for others to walk in the love of God, but never praying that for ourselves.

He was not self-seeking, but rather he was seeking Father God for his complete destiny. He escaped the identity that was placed on him by his own mother that was limiting his life through existing pain. Limitations set over our lives by our parents are the toughest ones to break—it requires the love and presence of Father God.

Jabez called on Father God. He desired to live a life of honor. He honored Father God by making Him the source of everything he desired. He sowed honor in his prayer and received honor in his life.

Father God honored the direct request of Jabez for *more*. Let's venture to risk a life of *more*! There is *more* each of us can experience in this life. Make a direct request of Father God— like Jabez. Father God delights in shifting our identity with His honor, shattering the limitations pain has created.

It is our time to enter into His greater purposes for our lives with new assignments. Father God designs *more* for us to bring Him *more* glory in the earth. *More* is a prayer away.

SHATTERING THE LIMITATIONS OF PAIN

Declarations: Please lift your hands above your head in victory while speaking out loud these declarations and experience the shift Father God brings.

I was created by You, Father God, to win. Sin brought loss, but I was born again to win again.

Father God, I thank you for empowering me in my destiny assignments to release victories for others.

I was formed by Your genius to fit my destiny; a life of success, influence and purpose.

Father God, Your present love and future promises elevate my vision and faith.

My identity is filled with Your love and honor.

Bless me to release Your love and honor to others today.

I embrace Your greatness in my life and I ask that You enlarge my territory.

My praise is from You, Father, not from men. I am learning to hear it and live in it.

You are sending people whose voices carry Your voice to encourage me.

More is possible for me because You are *more*, You do *more*, and You designed me in Your image for *more*.

I will believe *more*, think *more*, dream *more*, and live *more*. Let my life bring You *more* glory.

Father God, you are the delight of my heart. Living my life of destiny is a part of my worship to you.

Father God, bless my identity—bless my *"me."* Every curse spoken over my *"me"* by others or myself, are breaking by Your words of truth and blessing.

Father God, show Yourself strong through of me.

Your life is in me and my life is in You and that is unlocking the anointing, gifts, and abilities that you formed in me for my purpose.

Your favor rests over me because I am Yours. Because I favor You and Your ways, Your favor over my life is increasing.

My kingdom identity reveals, empowers and defines my assignments that are expanding even as I am speaking.

You are giving me revelation concerning my purpose as I journey into my destiny.

The anointing on my life increases when I enter the assignments and purposes for which You created me.

I was made for this. You created me for this. My "this" brings You glory.

You created me to make You famous in a unique way to certain people groups in my generation—for such a time as this.

Every new thought You give me prepares and establishes me for an astounding new season.

Your heart is in my heart, Your words are in my words, Your thoughts are in my thoughts and Your ways are in my ways.

I am dreaming today with You, Father God, concerning my future and my purposes. Limits off—possibilities on—because of You.

I determine to live a life more honorable to You in the earth. I am shattering the limitations of pain—just like Jabez.

What is around me does not change my identity (who You made me), my identity changes what's around me.

As my identity grows in You, I have the privilege to change more difficult situations that impact more people.

This day is fruitful and miraculous because Your hand is with me.

My anointed identity is dreaming into my assignments You have given to me.

I am receiving wisdom, strategies, timing and direction from You.

I am attaining a quantum leap in my identity like Jabez and experiencing more because I am crying out to You, Father God.

Father God—bless me! Enlarge my territory! Let Your hand be with me! Keep me in Your presence and from evil! I decree I will not live in pain nor will I cause it! I receive "more" from You today.

Shattering the Limitations of Pain

"This book is a treasure...
it will change your life–guaranteed!"
-Dutch Sheets

AND
DAVID
PERCEIVED
HE WAS KING
IDENTITY - THE KEY TO YOUR DESTINY
DALE L. MAST

God took David from the fields where he followed the sheep to become the ruler of Israel. He was overlooked by his father, yet chosen by God. He carried the dream to be king from the day Samuel anointed him, but he did not feel worthy to marry the king's daughter after defeating Goliath. David experienced many amazing moments in his life, yet he also endured many traumas. He was the hero of Israel and then became the hunted villain. He went from leading the armies of Israel to being pursued by the same. When David was anointed king in Judah, civil war erupted. Each step that God was establishing David's identity, the enemy was trying to steal it. Defeating Goliath required faith, but taking the throne required identity. It takes a Goliath to reveal a David, and his journey to produce a king. Faith believes what God can do. Identity believes what God can do through you. Let David's journey touch yours.

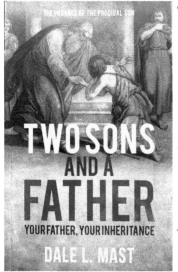

The prodigal son did not *want* to live in his father's presence. The older son did not know *how* to live in his father's presence. Both sons had the same problem—they desired fatherless parties. The younger son wasted his inheritance while the older brother slaved in the midst of his—trying to earn what he refused to receive. Asking is the privilege of sons, an authority hidden from orphans.

God, the creator of all mankind, desires to be your Father. When the disciples asked Jesus to teach them how to pray, the first two words He gave them, "Our Father," set the tone and reality of the entire prayer. If these two words do not grip our hearts, the rest of the words lose context as well as the implicit favor that comes from that dynamic personal relationship.

There are keys to receiving our inheritance that are absolutely necessary to fulfill our destiny. The prodigal was restored by his father's love and mercy, but it was his father's celebration that completed and empowered his life. Your best robe is in His closet. It's time to enter your Father's celebration!

Change does not come to earth, just because we believe – we must be willing to lead. Everything on the earth hinges on leadership. We are learning to live and lead from the throne of David—the heart and authority of God. The purpose of this book is to advance healthy leadership by understanding its value and purpose. Whatever we do not value we will discard or misuse.

Without leadership, great visions will never survive. Everyone who leads serves others, and everyone who serves is leading someone. Our lives were created to bring advancement to what already exists as well as pursuing that which has never been accomplished. David's anointed worship as a shepherd boy did not change Israel until he became king. Greater assignments are given as we address more significant challenges and problems with vision and leadership. When you lead, who you are shifts the world or someone's world. As long as you are alive—never stop leading, never stop dreaming and never stop loving—it's God's adventure for your life.

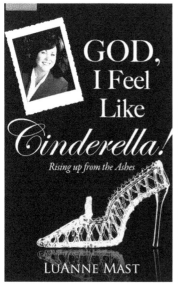

Sweeping the ashes out of the fireplace at my first job as a cleaning lady, I was overwhelmed. My husband of 23 years had left me for another woman, and I was thrust into the role of a struggling single mom. At that time my mother died of cancer, my house went foreclosure, my car was repossessed, and I was forced into unexpected bankruptcy. In frustration, I lifted my hands up to the Lord and cried out, "God, I feel like Cinderella!" He answered me right away. He said, "You are Cinderella, and I will redeem you!" I had already experienced the supernatural power of prayer, healings, and miracles. I was visited by an angel and prayed for a man that was raised from the dead. So when I heard God answer me in those ashes, I knew I had to trust Him like never before.

CPSIA information can be obtained
at www.ICGtesting.com
Printed in the USA
BVHW070831050221
598622BV00005B/8